# IN THE
# HOLY of HOLIES

An impassioned response to recent attacks
on the sanctuary and Ellen G. White

## CLIFFORD GOLDSTEIN

**Pacific Press® Publishing Association**
Nampa, Idaho
Oshawa, Ontario, Canada
www.pacificpress.com

Designed by Michelle C. Petz


Additional copies of this book are available by calling toll free 1-800-765-6955
or visiting http://www.adventistbookcenter.com


Unless otherwise noted, all scriptures are quoted from the King James Version.

Quotations attributed to the NIV are from the Holy Bible, New International Version.
Copyright © 1973, 1978, 1984, International Bible Society. Used by permission of
Zondervan Bible Publishers.

Quotations attributed to the NEB are from the New English Bible. Copyright © The
Delegates of the Oxford University Press and The Syndics of the Cambridge
University Press 1961, 1970. Used by permission.


Library of Congress Cataloging-in-Publication data:

Goldstein, Clifford.
Graffiti in  the holy of holies : An impassioned response to recent attacks
on the sanctuary and Ellen G. White / Clifford Goldstein.
p. cm.
Includes bibliographical references.
ISBN 0-8163-2007-1
1. Ratzlaff, Dale. Cultic doctrine of Seventh-day Adventists.
2. Seventh-day Adventists—Apologetic works. I. Title.

BX6154.R383G65 2004
230'.6732—dc22                                                        2003061661


05 06 07 • 5 4 3

# CONTENTS

To James Richardson and Scott Humphreys

# CHAPTER ONE

# THREE-LEGGED STOOLS

In the late 1980s, Pacific Press published *1844 Made Simple,*[1] a somewhat frenetic attempt by a new Adventist (yours truly) to defend the 1844 pre-Advent judgment. Since that time, I have learned so much more that has strengthened my belief, not only in the validity of our 1844 pre-Advent teaching but in its importance as well.

Many things have brought me to this point, one of them being that opponents of the doctrine not only have failed to come up with anything new to oppose it, they won't even confront our best defenses of it. One would think that, after so much time, they would have something original—something fresh—to level against what they so boldly disdain. Yet all they do is hurl the same arthritic arguments against the 1844 pre-Advent judgment: *What about the context problem of Daniel 8? There's no validity to the year-day principle. There's no verbal link between Daniel 8 and 9. Antiochus Epiphanes as the little horn, . . . and on and on.*

Of course, they claim that these arguments have never been answered. I disagree. In the 1980s and 1990s, the church, using its best theologians, published the *Daniel and Revelation Committee Series*—seven volumes of scholarly chapters that dealt with many of these challenges. However much they make fun of these books, the critics have never seriously refuted the material in them. Instead, they simply utter blanket condemnations of the series, and then move on.

Take the year-day principle, one of the bogeymen cited by those opposed to 1844. On more than one occasion I've heard a well-known critic claim that "there's not a modicum of evidence of the year-day principle in the Bible." Fine. But instead of mocking the *Daniel and Revelation Committee Series* (which he has done), why has he never confronted the two chapters in the series that defend the year-day principle? If the year-day principle isn't biblical, then instead of just attacking the doctrine, or mocking the books that defend it, why not debunk—point by point—this defense of it? I've never heard him, or anyone, even try.

It's not just the year-day principle, either. Despite the usual snorting and fuming against the series, why haven't critics tackled, point by point, its refutation of the Antiochus Epiphanes interpretation of Daniel 8? Or its refutation of the supposed context problem of Daniel 8? Or its powerful chapter on the pagan and papal aspects of the little horn? Or its defense of our position on Hebrews? With so many voices promoting the Antiochus interpretation for Daniel 8, one would think that at least one of these voices would challenge (or at least try to challenge) the church's best refutation of that interpretation. Instead, (as with the other chapters) there is nothing, which has led me to think that if the critics could refute these things they would, but *because they can't,* they don't—a silence that only strengthens my belief in the 1844 doctrine.

But, of course, even more affirming than their silence has been the Word of God itself. While some of these folks are trying to decide which parts of the Bible are correct and which aren't, my study of the Bible has continued to affirm my belief in the 1844 sanctuary message. Especially helpful has been my greater understanding and appreciation of the gospel in the context of the sanctuary and the judgment. This, with more study on Daniel, Revelation, and the Cross, has enhanced my belief in 1844 and the pre-Advent judgment.

Over the years, as I learned more, I kept thinking that I needed to get what I have learned in print—to update and fill out *1844 Made Simple.* After years of procrastinating, I finally did so, but only after being spurred on by something else.

That catalyst was a book called *The Cultic Doctrine of Seventh-day Adventists (CDSDA),* written and published by Dale Ratzlaff, a former Adventist minister who left the church in 1981 because he and his wife had, he wrote, "studied our way out."[2] Brother Ratzlaff—a fourth-generation Adventist educated in SDA schools from first grade through seminary—now runs Life Assurance Ministries (LAM), which has a specific outreach "to Seventh-day Adventists, inquiring Adventists, Sabbatarians and concerned Evangelicals."[3] LAM also has a publishing arm whose mission statement reads: "To write, publish, stock and sell books relevant to former Seventh-day Adventists, inquiring Adventists, Sabbatarians and concerned Evangelicals. Our goal is to become the source for accurate information on Adventist doctrine and practice for the Evangelical world."[4] Among the books LAM sells are titles from such luminaries as Desmond Ford, Walter Rea, Ron Numbers, Jerry Gladson, and Brother Ratzlaff himself (including *Sabbath in Crisis*, his attempt to debunk the Adventist position on the Sabbath). Though I wouldn't begin to judge the hearts or motives of these authors, and despite differences in tone, approach, and scholarship, these works (at least the ones I'm familiar with) share one commonality: criticism of either the Seventh-day Adventist Church, its leaders, Adventist doctrines (specifically 1844), and, of course, the ministry of Ellen G. White.

*Graffiti in the Holy of Holies* is my response to *The Cultic Doctrine of Seventh-day Adventists*. My interest here is not Brother Ratzlaff, his motives, sincerity, or integrity. Regarding him personally, I'm hoping that the words—"Judge not" (Matthew 7:1) and these, "True Christian love cherished in the heart and exemplified in the life, would teach us to put the best possible construction upon the course of our brethren"[5]—will be my guide. The vicissitudes of time have made such principles *somewhat* easier for me to follow because, still dealing with my own tenacious character defects, I'm less inclined to engage in philippics against those whose hearts I don't know and whose weaknesses might not be as heinous in the sight of God as my own. In fact, to give (admittedly) faint praise, Brother Ratzlaff has tackled some issues with a frank, even refreshing, bluntness. Unlike others, who—while either subtly or overtly condemning key teachings—still claim to be Adventists, Brother Ratzlaff has taken his premises to their logical conclusions. For example, Brother Ratzlaff writes: "To remove the cleansing of the heavenly sanctuary and the investigative judgment doctrine from SDA theology will bring into question the inspiration and authority of the writings of Ellen White and the integrity of the whole Adventist movement."[6]

I agree. And had I rejected the judgment as he has done, I would have left the Seventh-day Adventist Church as he did.

Nevertheless, those seeking to judge Brother Ratzlaff less generously could, if so inclined, find reasons to do so.

Take the section from page 43 to page 93 in *CDSDA*. In these three chapters Brother Ratzlaff claims that Ellen White comprehensively endorsed William Miller's theology, particularly Miller's fifteen "proofs" for fastening on the date 1843 (revised to 1844) for Christ's return.

Now, assume that you (like me) reject fourteen of those proofs, while you (like me) believe that one, the one derived from Daniel 8:14, is valid. There's still the problem of Ellen White's endorsement of the others because, as Brother Ratzlaff asserts, she sweepingly approved of Miller's methods and message: "We can see that Ellen White's endorsement of William Miller is comprehensive. It is of great importance to our study to realize that she unequivocally states that Miller was guided by God in his methods, his conclusions, and his message."[7]

He continues: "The foundation of Adventism is laid in Ellen White's comprehensive endorsement of William Miller's methods and message."[8]

And, again: "In the last chapter we saw that Ellen White gave William Miller a comprehensive, glowing endorsement. She, speaking with 'prophetic authority,' stated unequivocally that God chose Miller, guided his mind in the study of the Scriptures, and showed him a method of Bible interpretation which linked one part of Scripture to another in such a way as to help him discover a 'perfect chain of truth.' "[9]

Immediately after this last quote, Brother Ratzlaff examines Miller's methods, admonishing his readers "to take the needed time to *carefully read each of Miller's fifteen proofs. Examine his use of Scripture and his resulting conclusions. Without a thorough understanding of this chapter, it will be impossible to grasp the arguments and conclusions of this book.* This chapter locks in—or out—many of the unique aspects of Adventist theology, hermeneutics and the prophetic ministry of Ellen White (emphasis in the original)."[10]

Most Adventists, I imagine, would be surprised to discover that "many of the unique aspects" of our theology and hermeneutics can be found in Miller's proofs (or at least in fourteen of them) that 99.9 percent of us probably never heard of and certainly would not take seriously as proof for 1844 even if we did (apparently, William Miller, after finding a valid proof in Daniel, got a bit carried away).

Nevertheless, the crucial point is Brother Ratzlaff's challenge: Ellen White gave a comprehensive endorsement to Miller's methods, which included fifteen proofs for 1843 (1844). Ellen White, therefore, can hardly be a prophet—because what prophet could endorse such blatant error?

"The stakes are high for Adventists," writes Brother Dale. "If Miller was wrong, then Ellen White was equally wrong."[11]

Correct, except for one problem. After taking three chapters to construct the argument that, because she endorsed Miller's methods and proofs, Ellen White couldn't be a prophet—our dear brother, in a footnote at the bottom of the last page of the third chapter, writes: "It's not clear if Ellen White endorsed all of Miller's fifteen 'proofs.' "[12]

Now maybe I'm missing something here, but doesn't this footnote—which states that it's *not* clear if Ellen White endorsed all of Miller's fifteen proofs—give away the show? Was not the whole point of the previous fifty pages—thirty or more of which were used to critique Miller's fifteen proofs (proofs that readers were admonished to study carefully because without understanding them it *"will be impossible to grasp the arguments and conclusions of this book")*—to demonstrate that Ellen White's comprehensive endorsement of Miller's fifteen "proofs" gave evidence that she was a false prophet? *And yet he candidly states that he doesn't know for sure that she endorsed all these proofs?* Maybe, then, her "comprehensive" endorsement wasn't so "comprehensive" after all?

How did Brother Ratzlaff allow such an egregious contradiction into his book? Perhaps he didn't have a sharp editor. Perhaps, as often happens to me, you get so close to what you write you miss some problems in it (that is, until the day you see it in print). Or maybe realizing that his case wasn't so strong, perhaps Brother Ratzlaff felt moved by his conscience to express the truth, even if only in a footnote.

### THE ADVENTIST BIBLE

There is another place where, again, if one were inclined to judge Brother Ratzlaff harshly, one could do so. In a chapter titled "Tampering with the Word,"[13] he writes: "Some cults, such as the Mormons and Jehovah's Witnesses, have their own Bibles which they claim to be more accurate than other Bibles."[14] Then, in this context—that of the Mormon and Jehovah's Witnesses Bibles—he states that "the SDA community had come out with two new Bibles,"[15] the direct implication being that, like Mormons and Jehovah's Witnesses, Adventists have been "tampering with the Word" in order to support our doctrines.

What Bibles is he referring to which show that we are tampering with God's Word?

For starters, *The Clear Word.*

*The Clear Word?* Because a denominational press printed (as opposed to published) a paraphrase of the Bible, that denomination now has its own Bible in a manner akin to the Jehovah's Witnesses' *New World Trans-*

lation? (Because Penguin Books prints the Koran, is that company now Muslim?) Anyone who knows anything about Seventh-day Adventists knows how unfair and inaccurate the claim is that *The Clear World* is some sort of official Adventist version of the Bible.

I read a lot of material published by our church; rarely, if ever, do I see *The Clear Word* quoted, and the few times I have, it has always been referenced as a paraphrase. I edit the Adult Sabbath School Bible Study Guides (the "Quarterly"), the official denominational teaching publication for the world SDA Church; the publisher is the General Conference of Seventh-day Adventists. In the years that I have been in this job, not once has anyone ever quoted *The Clear Word* in a manuscript, and I would edit it out if they did, just as I would edit out any paraphrased version. And yet, according to Brother Ratzlaff, *The Clear Word* is evidence that we are "tampering with the Word" in order to support our teaching!

Most Adventists, I would guess, probably don't even own *The Clear Word* (I don't and probably never will, only because I have always disliked paraphrases, even one ostensibly tilted toward interpretations I would agree with). And of those Adventists who do own *The Clear Word,* most understand that it is a paraphrase, one person's *interpretation* of what the Bible says, and that it is not a study Bible, not something to learn doctrine from, and that it's no more the "Adventist Bible" than *The Message,* written by Eugene Peterson, is a "Presbyterian Bible."

The cover of *The Clear Word* expressly states that it is a paraphrase. The author begins the preface by saying: "This is not a new translation but a paraphrase of the Scriptures. It is not intended for in-depth study or for public reading in churches."[16]

It's not even published by an Adventist publishing house. Dr. Jack Blanco, the author, holds the copyright. The Review and Herald merely prints and distributes it; the book is not a Review and Herald publication. When first published it was called *The Clear Word Bible;* in later editions, to try to avoid misunderstanding, the title was changed to *The Clear Word,* an act that hardly bodes well for those who assert that the Seventh-day Adventist Church has its own Bible version.

The other example Brother Ratzlaff cites of Adventists "tampering with the Word" is *The Study Bible.*

The *what* Bible? Most Adventists, I imagine, have never heard of it. I hadn't—at least not until Brother Dale wrote in his book that it was another Adventist Bible.

So what is *The Study Bible*? A self-supporting school printed the King James Version with commentary by Ellen White in the margins, like the Scofield Reference Bible. As with *The Clear Word*, however, *The Study Bible* was only printed, not published, by the Review and Herald. In fact, when the school first approached the Ellen G. White Estate about the idea, its board voted unanimously *not* to endorse the project because it "would give critics apparent support for their claims that we accept Ellen White's writings as another Bible."[17] After the school published it anyway, the Ellen G. White Estate said in response:

> The fact that this study Bible has been provided to the Research Center should not be considered as an endorsement either of this publication or of any other that places the writings of Ellen G. White within the two covers of a Bible. Though we believe that Mrs. White was inspired by the same Spirit that inspired the Bible writers, we also believe that the canon of Scripture is closed, and that it is a disservice to Mrs. White and the church to blur the difference between her writings and those of the Bible. Any publication, however innocently conceived and produced, that makes it appear that the church considers Mrs. White's writings as part of the canon, opens the church to the charge of being a cult.[18]

For some reason, that quote didn't make it into Brother Ratzlaff's book. But then, he hasn't been in the Adventist Church since 1981. So long out of the loop, he perhaps didn't know these things. His lack of knowledge is, therefore, understandable. However, as Life Assurance Ministries seeks to be "the source for *accurate information* on Adventist doctrine and practice" (italics supplied)—these lapses reveal shoddy research, at best.

## THE CRUX OF THE MATTER

Of course, Brother Ratzlaff's charge of Adventists "tampering with the Word" isn't the real issue. His main charge, as presented in *The Cultic Doctrine of Seventh-day Adventists,* can be pared down to one sentence: *The doctrine of the investigative judgment is not biblical, and therefore Ellen White, who promoted that doctrine, is a false prophet.* Here, in twenty-one simple words, is his attack. And here, in your hands, is my response.

Only by understanding the structure of his attack can one understand my response to it. For instance, Brother Ratzlaff spends the first eight chapters of his book dealing with why he believes Ellen White was not a prophet; the rest of *CDSDA* deals with the investigative judgment. I'm going to reverse that order in my response because, to put it simply, if the investigative judgment isn't biblical, then the issue regarding Ellen White is moot. If you can debunk the judgment, why bother with her? To use an analogy: If you can disprove the existence of God, why bother rebutting justification by faith alone?

I can accept that Ellen White, even as a prophet, was fallible, both in her life and writings. Her prophetic ministry, in my thinking, is not diminished if she made mistakes, grew in her understanding of doctrine and theology, changed her mind on doctrinal and theological issues, even, at one point, had an erroneous view of the Sabbath or of the law in Galatians, or didn't fully understand some of her own visions. I can accept that her humanity intruded upon her work and ministry (tell me that Moses', John the Baptist's, or Peter's didn't intrude upon theirs). Inspiration doesn't automatically include inerrancy. What I can't accept, however, considering the importance she placed upon the teaching of the pre-Advent judgment, is that she could be a prophet and be wrong about that. Maybe others can; I can't. Fortunately, I don't have to.

The issue is not Ellen White, though Brother Dale tries to make it her; the issue is the pre-Advent judgment. If the judgment is wrong, then she is wrong; and if she's wrong on *that*, her prophetic ministry should come under severe questioning. On the other hand, if the judgment is biblical, although that hardly proves her prophetic gift, it does at least gut the essence of Brother Dale's attack on her prophetic ministry.

For this reason, I start not with Ellen White but with the judgment. If Brother Ratzlaff is correct, and the teaching is not biblical, then there's no need to proceed with her because she can't be biblical either.

As Seventh-day Adventists, we are not (or at least we had better not be) sitting on a three-legged stool, one of those legs being Ellen White. Our foundation must be rooted in the Bible, and the Bible alone. I've been amazed, and pained, to see people almost lose their entire Christian experience because their faith in her ministry has been shaken, usually out of false assumptions regarding what inspiration means.

Thus, we deal first with the question of the judgment, and Brother Ratzlaff's criticism of it. Afterward, we look at his attacks on Ellen White.

Also, however much he may be mentioned in this book, Brother Ratzlaff is not the issue. Ideas, not the persons behind those ideas, are. Our brother is, in fact, a victim of mistakes, however unintentional, that most of us in the church have been victimized by to one degree or another, whether we know it or not. If time should last, more Dale Ratzlaffs will come and go, making the same charges, just as more Clifford Goldsteins will come and go, defending against those charges. We're looking at something that transcends people, or at least individuals—and that is biblical truths, which by their nature exist regardless of how anyone relates to them.

Though I will use Brother Ratzlaff's book as the basis for my response, the issues go beyond it. As I said in the opening pages, *Graffiti in the Holy of Holies*, though focusing on Brother Ratzlaff's attack, is essentially *1844 Made Simple* fleshed out and expanded in directions further than the original book went. Even if *CDSDA* hadn't been written, this material should have been presented because it deals with the heart and soul of what makes us Adventists. It's too bad this defense has to be done in the context of *CDSDA*, but "all things work together for good to them that love God, to them who are the called according to his purpose" (Romans 8:28). My hope, and prayer, is that through *Graffiti in the Holy of Holies* this will be one case where that biblical principle is clearly manifested.

---

[1] Goldstein, Clifford. *1844 Made Simple* (Pacific Press®, Nampa) 1988.

[2] Ratzlaff, Dale. *The Cultic Doctrine of Seventh-day Adventists* (Life Assurance Ministries; Glendale, Arizona) 1996, p. 13.

[3] Taken from *www.LifeAssuranceMinistries.com* (January 26, 2001).

[4] *Ibid.* (January 26, 2001).

[5] Ellen White. *Review and Herald*, April 15, 1880, par. 12.

[6] *CDSDA*, p. 20.

[7] *Ibid.*, p. 49.

[8] *Ibid.*, p. 43.

[9] *Ibid.*, p. 52.

[10] *Ibid.*, p. 54 (italics Ratzlaff's).

[11] *Ibid.*, p. 52.

[12] *Ibid.*, p. 93. cf. p. 28.

[13] *Ibid.*, p. 303.

[14] *Ibid.*, p. 303, 304.

[15] *Ibid.*, p. 304.

[16] Jack Blanco, *The Clear Word* © 1994 Jack J. Blanco. Printed and distributed by the Review and Herald Publishing Association, Hagerstown, MD, p. vii.

[17] Ellen G. White Estate Board. Minutes (September 30, 1990).

[18] Ellen G. White Estate Board of Trustees, September 1998.

# CHAPTER TWO

# SLIVER

## IN THE

# FOOT

In *The Cultic Doctrine of Seventh-day Adventists*, Dale Ratzlaff calls the investigative judgment a "sliver in the foot" of Adventism. However, because I agree with him that "the doctrine of the cleansing of the heavenly sanctuary and the investigative judgment is indeed 'the foundation and central pillar of Adventism,' "[1]—then if that doctrine is wrong it's not a sliver in the foot but a dagger in the heart.

Before we keel over dead, though, a fascinating element in *CDSDA* must be addressed.

"The cleansing of the heavenly sanctuary and the investigative judgment," Brother Dale writes, "*as a continuing doctrine*, is the legacy of Ellen White and no one else"[2] (italics his). One could debate this charge; I intend, in fact, to debunk it.

Again (and it can't be stressed enough), Ellen White is not the key issue; that she has been made so says something about how poorly our church has presented her ministry and the doctrine of the pre-Advent judgment (more about that later). The only issue is this: Can the pre-Advent judgment itself be supported by Scripture? Once that's answered, everything else falls into place.

Our brother's book claims to be an attack on the doctrine of the pre-Advent judgment, which it is. However, in a work that consumes about 380 pages, only one short chapter deals *specifically* with the biblical teaching of the pre-Advent judgment itself, and that chapter is only about fifteen pages long. Though Brother Ratzlaff touches on aspects of it from a "biblical" perspective here and there all through his tome, most of the book is about Ellen White, William Miller, the "shut door," the *Clear Word*, and so forth. A book purporting to show why the doctrine of the pre-Advent judgment is not biblical would have, ideally, concentrated more heavily on the specific biblical teaching. That's not, however, the essence of *CDSDA*.

Why? One can only guess. However, there's no question that this disproportion of material stems partly from the misconception, common among many Adventist members still, that the doctrine is "the legacy of Ellen White and no one else." Also, it's easier and safer to deal with fallible beings and entities like Ellen White, William Miller, and the Adventist Church than with the biblical texts themselves. For whatever reason, the one concentrated attempt to debunk the doctrine itself, specifically from the Bible, is in chapter 10, "A Broken Chain."[3]

Much of my response to our brother's book will center heavily on this chapter because it's pivotal. If I can't undo the arguments here, there's no sense bothering with Ellen White, the "shut door," and the rest. On the other hand, if I can build the case here, the rest is (or should be) gravy.

Another point needs to be addressed as well, which I touched on in the first chapter. An incredible amount of scholarly work has been invested in answering arguments brought against the pre-Advent judgment, much having been done after our brother left the church. So, ideally, he could be excused for not knowing about this research. However, the appendix of *CDSDA* contains a "Select Bibliography"[4] that lists most of these works, such as the seven volumes of the Daniel and Revelation Committee Series, composed of almost 2,000 pages by dozens of our best theologians, all written to deal either directly or indirectly with the common charges made against the investigative judgment, charges that our brother levels in *CDSDA*. Brother Ratzlaff knew about the books and yet, for whatever reason, chose to ignore the arguments in them—arguments that would (I contend) debunk his thesis regarding the pre-Advent judgment. If he would have confronted some of those books, or at least the sections that deal with the charges he makes, and then sought to rebut them, point by point (as I will to do to his work)—that approach, if nothing else, would have been more credible than merely listing a string of arguments against the judgment while ignoring their best defense.

Though ignoring that material, Brother Dale writes that, "a few, clear Bible references are more than enough to show, beyond the shadow of a doubt, that the doctrine of the cleansing of the heavenly sanctuary and the investigative judgment is not supported by Scripture and is contrary to it at almost every point."[5] That's quite a bold statement, one that any serious Adventist needs to look at.

Thus, the next few chapters will examine these "few, clear Bible references" that "beyond the shadow of a doubt" prove not only that the pre-Advent judgment is wrong, but that it is contrary to Scripture "at almost every point." For if these texts say what our brother claims, they would not be a sliver in the foot but, as I said, a dagger in the heart.

[1] *CDSDA*, p. 265.
[2] *Ibid.*, p. 19.
[3] *Ibid.*, p. 165.
[4] *Ibid.*, Appendix D. pp. 377–383.
[5] *Ibid.*, pp. 165, 167.

# CHAPTER THREE

# THE

# ANTIOCHUS

# EPIPHANY

Any attack on the 2,300-day prophecy should center on the key text behind it—Daniel 8:14. "And he said unto me, Unto two thousand and three hundred days; then shall the sanctuary be cleansed" (KJV). This is exactly what Brother Dale does—attack us on this text. If successful, if he can prove that we have misinterpreted it, we're toast.

Thus, we will look at Daniel 8:14, at our interpretation of it, and then examine his attack on that interpretation. Only then can we evaluate the validity of his charges.

To begin, Daniel 8 (the chapter containing the controverted verse) consists of two parts—a vision and then an explanation (at least partially) of that vision. The first fourteen verses, ending with Daniel 8:14 (the vision about the 2,300 days) compose the vision itself; verses 15-27 deal with the explanation of the vision. Many Bibles break up the chapter into two sections with added space between verses 14 and 15, often with a subtitle over the second part, a division that doesn't appear in the Hebrew itself.

After being given the vision, Daniel didn't understand it (Daniel 8:15); then he hears a voice say to Gabriel, "Make this man to understand the vision" (verse 16). In other words, someone (presumably the Lord; after all, who else orders Gabriel around?) tells Gabriel to make Daniel understand what he had just seen. Gabriel, obeying, then comes to Daniel and says, "Understand, O son of man: for at *the time of the end shall be the vision*" (verse 17, italics supplied). Gabriel then says, "Behold I will make thee know what shall be in the *last end* of the indignation: for *at the time appointed the end* shall be" (verse 19, italics supplied). Finally, Gabriel's last words of explanation to Daniel are, "And the vision of the evening and the morning which was told is true: wherefore shut thou up the vision; for it shall be *for many days*" (verse 26, italics supplied).

Without looking at the vision or the interpretation, we can see that whatever this vision is, it deals with a period of time Gabriel calls "the end," "the time of the end," or "last end." What does that mean? When Gabriel, having spoken to Daniel six centuries before Christ, talks about "the time of the end" or the "last end"—what is he referring to? Does he mean "the end" as we, Seventh-day Adventists, living thousands of years after Daniel 8 was written, understand "the end"? Are we justified in automatically placing our perspective regarding time on something written so long ago?

Of course not, at least not automatically. Instead, the book of Daniel itself gives some powerful evidence that can help us understand the meaning of these phrases *in their particular context*. Only then can we better understand what they mean and whether that meaning fits with our understanding of "the end."

## DANIEL CHAPTERS 2, 7, AND 8

Daniel 8 has many similarities to both Daniel 2 and Daniel 7. Unlike Daniel 1, and Daniel 3–6—which are composed of narratives telling specific stories in a local, regional context (Daniel and the three Hebrews refusing the king's food, Nebuchadnezzar's golden image, the king losing his mind, Belshazzar's feast, Daniel in the lions' den)—Daniel 2, 7, and 8 deal with much broader topics (and cover a much longer time span) than the mere foibles and successes of a handful of people, captives and kings in ancient Babylon and Media-Persia.

Chapters 2, 7, 8, unlike the narrative chapters, consist of two basic parts: a dream (Daniel 2; 7) or a vision (Daniel 8), then an interpretation of that dream or vision that points specifically to the rise and fall of various empires beyond the local politics of the time in which the vision or dream itself occurred. Thus, by the similarity of their structure, theme, and context, these three chapters not only stand out from the rest of those early chapters, but they exist in close relationship to each other.[1] By looking at all three we can learn more about each one.

For instance, in chapter 2, Daniel—getting light directly from heaven

(Daniel 2:19-23)—interprets the king's dream. According to what the Lord had told him, Daniel recounts world history, starting with Babylon itself (Daniel 2:38) and concluding with the end of the world, at least as the world is now constituted.

How do we know? After describing the demise of the last earthly kingdom, the fourth, which breaks up into small, lesser kingdoms prior to the end (Daniel 2:40-44), Daniel concludes his interpretation of the king's dream with these words:

> And in the days of these kings shall the God of heaven set up a kingdom, which shall never be destroyed: and the kingdom shall not be left to other people, but it shall break in pieces and consume all these kingdoms, and it shall stand for ever. Forasmuch as thou sawest that the stone was cut out of the mountain without hands, and that it brake in pieces the iron, the brass, the clay, the silver, and the gold; the great God hath made known to the king what shall come to pass hereafter: and the dream is certain, and the interpretation thereof sure (Daniel 2:44-45, KJV).

What did the Lord show Daniel here? (Remember: Daniel is simply recounting what God gave him in a "night vision.") When do the sequences of events depicted in the dream end?

In the dream itself, the king saw an image whose head was gold, whose breast and arms were silver, whose belly and thighs were brass, whose legs were iron, and whose feet were iron and clay (Daniel 2:31-33). These, of course, represent various world empires (Daniel 2:38-40), given in the chronological order in which they appeared. What happens after them?

> Thou sawest till that a stone was cut out without hands, which smote the image upon his feet that were of iron and clay, and brake them to pieces. Then was the iron, the clay, the brass, the silver, and the gold, broken to pieces together, and became like the chaff of the summer threshing-floors; and the wind carried them away, that no place was found for them: and the stone that smote the image became a great mountain, and filled the whole earth. This is the dream (Daniel 2:34-36).

In other words, what Daniel said in verses 44-46 about the God of heaven setting up an eternal kingdom that would break and consume all the previous ones, is the interpretation of these verses here (34-36), which deal with the stone "cut out without hands" that smashes the previous kingdoms to the point where "no place was found for them" (Daniel 2:35).

Daniel 2, starting in the reign of Babylon, covers a time frame that concludes sometime in the future beyond our day (much less Daniel's) with God Himself setting up an eternal kingdom.

In Daniel 2:45, the prophet says to the king that "the great God hath made known to [thee] what shall come to pass *hereafter*" (Daniel 2:45, italics supplied). The NAS translates this phrase as what "will take place in the future." The Aramaic word, *acharay*, "hereafter" or "future," comes from the same basic root, *achr*, translated from the Hebrew in 8:19 as "the latter end." Both Daniel 2 and Daniel 8 deal with the *achr*, and Daniel 2 proves that the *achr*, the end (at least in this chapter) includes the end of the world as we, Seventh-day Adventists, understand it—the demise of all earthly kingdoms after Jesus returns.

Parallel to Daniel 2 is Daniel 7, another chapter composed of a supernatural revelation (a dream) and a supernatural interpretation. As in Daniel 2, there's another sequence of world history depicting the rise and fall of four great empires followed by the establishment of God's kingdom. In fact, the interpretation starts out with these words: "These great beasts, which are four, are four kings, which shall arise out of the earth. But the saints of the most High shall take the kingdom, and possess the kingdom for ever, even for ever and ever" (Daniel 7:17, 18), a statement that undeniably places the end of the chapter into the Second Coming and beyond. As in Daniel 2, there will be four great empires, but in the end God will establish an eternal kingdom.

In the vision, Daniel sees four beasts arise out of the sea (Daniel 7:3)—a lion, a bear, a leopard, a fourth beast, and then a horn power that arises out of the fourth beast (Daniel 7:4-8). Daniel then has a vision of a heavenly judgment scene (verses 9, 10, 13) that ultimately ends in God establishing an eternal kingdom. "And there was given him dominion, and glory, and a kingdom, that all people, nations, and languages, should serve him: his dominion is an everlasting dominion, which shall not pass away, and his kingdom that which shall not be destroyed" (Daniel 7:14). The vision of Daniel 7 itself ends with the establishment of this kingdom.

Though that part of the vision is clear, the interpretation reiterates the same idea. It focuses particularly on the activity of the little-horn power that arises out of the fourth beast and which is part of the fourth beast (Daniel

7:19-25). And then the explanation concludes with these words: "But the judgment shall sit, and they shall take away his dominion, to consume and to destroy it unto the end. And the kingdom and dominion, and the great-ness of the kingdom under the whole heaven, shall be given to the people of the saints of the most High, whose kingdom is an everlasting kingdom, and all dominions shall serve and obey him" (Daniel 7:26, 27).

If this isn't the end of our present world, what is?

Verse 26 concludes with these words: "to consume and destroy it *unto the end*" (italics supplied). Though the Aramaic root used here for "the end" isn't the same as the one found in Daniel 2:45 and 8:19, neverthe-less it makes the same point: In both Daniel 2 and Daniel 7, "the end" is depicted as we understand it—the demise of this world that results from the second coming of Christ.

Also, though both Daniel 2 and 7 deal with powers present at the time Daniel was writing (or which would soon arise), when the chapters refer to things that "shall come to pass" (Daniel 2:29) or events that shall be in the "hereafter" or "the future" (Daniel 2:45), this definitely includes events future not only to Daniel himself, but to us as well.

Daniel 8, like Daniel 2 and Daniel 7, consists of a supernatural revela-tion and a supernatural explanation. As does its two predecessors, it deals with various world empires. Though Daniel 2 and 7 began with Babylon (Daniel 2:38 even names it), depicting three other powers that follow in succession finally ending with God's kingdom, Daniel 8 depicts only three powers. It doesn't include Babylon (probably because by the time Daniel had the vision that is recorded in chapter 8, Babylon was soon to fade). Instead, the vision consists of a ram (Daniel 8:3, 4), a goat (verses 5-8), a little horn (verses 9-12), and then the sanctuary being cleansed (verse 14). According to the interpretation of the vision, the ram is Media-Persia, which is named (verse 20); the goat is Greece, which is named (verse 21); and the little horn, though unnamed, is depicted as an oppressive, vio-lent, and deceitful power ultimately destroyed "without hand" (Daniel 8:25). Specifics about the sanctuary being cleansed are not given, even though Daniel was told that the vision in verse 14 about the 2,300 days and the cleansing of the sanctuary was true (verse 26).

Despite other commonalties, all three chapters share this point as well: *They end with the supernatural intervention of God.* Daniel 2 concludes with the stone cut out "without hands" (Daniel 2:45) that smites the image and crushes it, God's kingdom then being set up in its place. Daniel 7 ends with a judgment scene in heaven that ultimately leads to the demise of the little horn and the establishment of God's kingdom (Daniel 7:25-28). Daniel 8 ends with the little horn being destroyed, according to 8:25, "without hand" ("not by human power" [NIV]), followed by some words about the vision of verse 14 being true and that the vision (probably referring to the entire chapter) should be shut up because "it shall be for many days" (verse 26).

Now, to return to our initial questions: *When Gabriel, having spoken to Daniel six centuries before Christ, talks about "the time of the end" or just "the end"—what is he referring to? Does he mean "the end" as we Seventh-day Adventists, living thousands of years after Daniel 8 was written, understand "the end"? Are we justified in automatically placing our perspective on something written so long ago?*

As I said earlier, no—we're not *automatically* justified in assuming that "the end" in Daniel means the same as when we talk about "the end." However, when looking at the evidence, particularly at the parallel chapters, one could indeed be justified in concluding that, just as Daniel 2 and Daniel 7 come to the "time of the end" as we understand it, Daniel 8 does as well.

Each chapter presents a sequence of military/political powers, the final one ultimately meeting its demise through the supernatural intervention of God. After displaying a series of political and military powers, Daniel 2 ends with the supernatural action of God. After displaying a series of political and military powers, Daniel 7 ends with the supernatural action of God. After displaying a series of political and military powers, Daniel 8 ends with the supernatural action of God. And, just as Daniel 2 and Daniel 7 deal with the end of the world, Daniel 8 does as well. When Daniel is told twice (Daniel 8:17, 19) that the chapter deals with "the end," it's not a stretch—particularly given the parallels with Daniel 2 and Daniel 7 which deal unmistakably with the end of the world—to see that "the end" in Daniel 8 is the same as "the end" in Daniel 2 and 7: the end of the present world.

| Daniel 2 | Daniel 7 | Daniel 8 |
|---|---|---|
| Earthly powers (verses 37-43) | Earthly powers (verses 17-25) | Earthly powers (verses 20-25) |
| Supernatural intervention of God (verse 44) | Supernatural intervention of God (verses 26-28) | Supernatural intervention of God (verse 25) |

## DANIEL 12

More evidence from Daniel 12 verifies this conclusion that "the end" in Daniel 8 refers to "the end" yet future even to us. A cursory reading of the chapter shows that it, too, is dealing (among other things) with the end of the world as we understand it. "At that time shall Michael stand up, the great prince which standeth for the children of thy people: and there shall be a time of trouble, such as never was since there was a nation even to that same time: and at that time thy people shall be delivered, every one that shall be found written in the book" (Daniel 12:1).

The concept of a "time of trouble, such as never was since there was a nation even to that same time" is generally understood as being yet in the future, an event that includes names being "found written" in "the book" . . . the book of life, perhaps (see Phillippians 4:3; Revelation 3:5; 13:8; 20:12, 15; 21:27; 22:19).

"And many of them that sleep in the dust of the earth shall awake, some to everlasting life, and some to shame and everlasting contempt" (Daniel 12:2). This is an unmistakable reference to something that is future even to us.

"But thou, O Daniel, shut up the words, and seal the book, even to the time of the end: many shall run to and fro, and knowledge shall be increased" (Daniel 12:4). The phrase "the time of the end" is the same as in Daniel 8:17 (the Hebrew vocalization is slightly different but due only to an accent shift that has no impact on meaning); and with "the time of the end" in Daniel 12 clearly including events future even to us, it's no radical stretch to believe that "the time of the end" in Daniel 8 does the same.

Also, in Daniel 12:4, Daniel is told to "shut up the words and seal the vision, even to the time of the end." In Daniel 8:26 Gabriel says to Daniel, "Shut thou up the vision; for it shall be for many days." These are parallel thoughts that imply (if nothing else) another link between Daniel 8 and Daniel 12, the latter being a chapter with undeniable end-time implications.

"And I heard, but I understood not: then said I, O my Lord, what shall be the end of these things? And he said, Go thy way, Daniel: for the words are closed up and sealed till the time of the end. . . . But go thou thy way till the end be: for thou shalt rest, and stand in thy lot at the end of the days" (Daniel 12:8, 9, 13).

In verse 9, Gabriel tells Daniel that the words are closed and sealed till "the time of the end," words that present another parallel to Daniel 8. In fact, the phrase here in verse 9, "the time of the end," is the same as in Daniel 12:4 and in 8:17. In Daniel 12:13, however, where the word "end" is used twice (it's the same word used for "end" in Daniel 8:17), it's the context that's most interesting. Daniel will stand in his lot "at the end of days," a clear reference to the resurrection of the dead at the end of the world, and thus more evidence that places some events in Daniel 8 in the future even to us.

Thus, the linguistic, structural, and semantic parallels between Daniel 2, 7, and 8 (which clearly deal with the end as we know it), as well as the linguistic ties and semantic parallels between Daniel 8 and Daniel 12 (which also deal with the end as we understand it), indicate that Daniel 8 is, in fact, dealing with "the end" as Adventists understand "the end."

The importance of this conclusion will be seen shortly.

One other point before carefully examining Brother Ratzlaff's attack on our interpretation of Daniel 8:14. As we've seen, Daniel 2, 7, and 8 have striking parallels in structure and content: (1) dream/vision followed by an explanation; (2) a survey of historical powers; and (3) the supernatural intervention of God.

But there's another parallel. Daniel 2 deals with an *unbroken sequence* of historical powers that ends with the supernatural intervention of God. Daniel 7 is the same: *an unbroken sequence* of powers ending with a massive judgment scene in heaven that concludes with the supernatural intervention of God. Daniel 8, as well, consists of an *unbroken sequence* of powers that ends with the supernatural intervention of God. In other words, each chapter displays a continuous chronological stream, a linear progression that starts in antiquity (at least 600 years before Christ), and flows, with no break, up through the supernatural act of God that, unmistakably in Daniel 2 and 7 (and by parallel Daniel 8) leads to the establishment of His kingdom, an event yet to happen.

The purpose of this point, as well, will be seen shortly.

## THE (LITTLE) HORN OF A DILEMMA

Now, let's take our first look at what Brother Dale says are "a few, clear Bible references [that] are enough to show, beyond the shadow of a doubt, that the doctrine of the cleansing of the sanctuary and the investigative judgment is not supported by Scripture and is contrary to it at almost every point."[2]

Brother Ratzlaff begins his "biblical evaluation" of the 2,300 days, of course, at Daniel 8. With the first part of the vision and its interpretation, he presents no challenge. The ram and the goat are named in Daniel: The ram is Media-Persia (Daniel 8:20) and the he-goat is Greece (verse 21). In the vision, the goat has a great horn that is broken, and four other powers come out of that horn (Daniel 8:5-8, 21, 22). To quote Brother Dale: "The large horn represented its first king, Alexander the Great. The four horns represented four kingdoms which would arise from Alexander's nation, although not with his power. Up to this point all evangelicals, even Seventh-day Adventists, are agreed that the four horns represent the four divisions of Alexander's empire."[3]

Thus, according to our brother, even Seventh-day Adventists have this right. The big issue comes next. In Daniel's vision, he saw a ram (which is Media-Persia), a goat that has a great horn which is broken in four parts (Greece and the break up of Greece after Alexander's death), and then comes the third major player in the vision, a terrible little-horn power that consumes much of the vision. It's depicted like this:

> And out of one of them came forth a little horn, which waxed exceeding great toward the south, and toward the east, and toward the pleasant land. And it waxed great, even to the host of heaven; and it cast down some of the host and of the stars to the ground, and stamped upon them. Yea, he magnified himself even to the prince of the host, and by him the daily sacrifice was taken away, and the place of his sanctuary was cast down. And an host was given him against the daily sacrifice by reason of transgression, and it cast down the truth to the ground, and it practised, and prospered (Daniel 8:9-12).

Here's the explanation that Gabriel gives to Daniel about the little-horn power:

> And in the latter time of their kingdom, when the transgressors are come to the full, a king of fierce countenance, and understanding dark sentences, shall stand up. And his power shall be mighty, but not by his own power: and he shall destroy wonderfully, and shall prosper, and practise, and shall destroy the mighty and the holy people. And through his policy also he shall cause craft to prosper in his hand; and he shall magnify himself in his heart, and by peace shall destroy many: he shall also stand up against the Prince of princes; but he shall be broken without hand (verses 23-25).

The question now arises: Who or what is this little horn? The answer is crucial, because here is where Brother Dale claims to confront "head on" the "sliver"[4] in the Adventist doctrine of the judgment. If he's correct here, there's no reason to proceed because we're dead in the water!

Before giving either our interpretation or Brother Dale's, let's define as many of the little horn's characteristics as possible, and from these, attempt to derive its identity (or at least to eliminate the false ones). We will look at the texts and then list the characteristics they give of the horn power—characteristics that the Lord deemed important enough to put in the vision of Daniel 8. In fact, more details are given about this little-horn power than about the other two powers in Daniel 8, an interesting point that might itself help identify it. Great emphasis is placed not only on the description of the little horn and its activities, but also on the explanation of this horn and those activities.

For example, in the interpretation one verse is used for Media-Persia (verse 20), while two are used for Greece, Alexander the Great, and the break up of the Grecian Empire into four kingdoms (verses 21, 22). These three verses cover the period from the middle-to-late sixth century B.C.— the rise of Media-Persia up through Alexander the Great (who died in 323 B.c).— and finally the four subsequent kingdoms that eventually dissipated under Roman hegemony in the second century B.C. Three verses cover almost 400 years. In comparison, the interpretation of the little horn *alone* takes three verses itself (verses 23-25). Though one shouldn't read too much into this fact, one shouldn't ignore it either. Whatever or whoever this power is, it's an entity of apparent historical significance, considering the space expended on it in contrast to either the Medo-Persian or Grecian behemoths, two highly important historical powers in and of themselves (more on this later).

Now, as previously seen, Daniel 8 doesn't appear in a vacuum, but comes with numerous parallels to Daniel 2 and Daniel 7, parallels that can help us identify the little horn.

Daniel 2, as we saw, starts out in the reign of Babylon (Daniel 2:26-38) and then is followed by a succession of three other kingdoms that arise before the world ends with God setting up His final kingdom (Daniel 2:39-45). The parallel between Daniel 2 and Daniel 8 shows that the two kingdoms following Babylon in chapter 2 are Media-Persia and Greece (Daniel 2:39; 8:20, 21). In fact, between the two chapters, three of these kingdoms are mentioned by name: Babylon, Media-Persia, then Greece—and they appeared, historically, in this exact chronological order. Thus the sequence in Daniel 2 is like this:

## Daniel 2
Babylon
Media-Persia
Greece
Final earthly kingdom
God's eternal kingdom

Again, this interpretation isn't unique to Adventism. The prophecy has been understood this way by commentators, both Jewish and Christian, for hundreds of years, if not longer.

Now, in Daniel 2 the final earthly kingdom that comes after Greece is symbolized in the statue as the iron that begins in the legs and extends to the feet and toes, where the iron is mixed with clay. The vision then clearly states that it is during this time, that of the iron and clay in the feet and toes, when God will set up His eternal kingdom:

> And as the toes of the feet were part of iron, and part of clay, so the kingdom shall be partly strong, and partly broken. And whereas thou sawest iron mixed with miry clay, they shall mingle themselves with the seed of men: but they shall not cleave one to another, even as iron is not mixed with clay. *And in the days of these kings shall the God of heaven set up a kingdom,* which shall never be destroyed: and the kingdom shall not be left to other people, but it shall break in pieces and consume all these kingdoms, and it shall stand forever (Daniel 2:42-44, italics supplied).

Now, the point's simplicity shouldn't mask its importance in helping us (later) identify the little horn of Daniel 8, and the point is this: Whatever the identity of the kingdom depicted in Daniel 2 by the iron which extends all the way to the end even if the form changes (clay is added to the iron in the feet and toes, though it's still iron all the way through)—this power is depicted not only as a powerful violent entity (Daniel 2:40) but as a kingdom that arises after Greece and extends to the end, when it is destroyed "without hands" (Daniel 2:34, 45) just as the little-horn power in Daniel 8 is destroyed "without hand" (Daniel 8:25).

Thus, whatever the fourth power is in Daniel 2, it arises after Greece, which is symbolized by the brass in the statue (Daniel 2:32, 34), and continues until God's final kingdom is established (Daniel 2:39-44). If this final power arose among the ruins of the Greek Empire, which collapsed before Christ and if it will continue until the Second Coming, then we're dealing with something of great longevity, as in thousands of years.

The same principle applies to the last earthly power of Daniel 7, another chapter that parallels Daniel 2 and Daniel 8. As in Daniel 2, Daniel 7 deals with a sequence of four empires followed by the establishment of God's kingdom after the last one. "These great beasts, which are four, are four kings, which shall arise out of the earth. But the saints of the most High shall take the kingdom, and possess the kingdom for ever, even for ever and ever" (Daniel 7:17, 18).

Again, the identity of the first three kingdoms—Babylon, Media-Persia, and Greece—are, for the most part, not in dispute. Thanks to Daniel 2 and Daniel 8, they have been clearly identified. In the vision, the fourth power— the last earthly one (just as in Daniel 2)—comes up after Greece and extends to the time of the end when God sets up His eternal kingdom:

> These great beasts, which are four, are four kings, which shall arise out of the earth. But the saints of the most High shall take the kingdom, and possess the kingdom for ever, even for ever and ever. Then I would know the truth of the fourth beast, which was diverse from all the others, exceeding dreadful, whose teeth were of iron, and his nails of brass; which devoured, brake in pieces, and stamped the residue with his feet; And of the ten horns that were in his head, and of the other which came up, and before whom three fell; even of that horn that had eyes, and a mouth that spake very great things, whose look was more stout than his fellows. I beheld, and the same horn made war with the saints, and prevailed against them; Until the Ancient of days came, and judgment was given to the saints of the most High; and the time came that the saints possessed the kingdom (Daniel 7:17-22).

So important, apparently, is this last earthly kingdom that more information is given in the interpretation:

> Thus he said, The fourth beast shall be the fourth kingdom upon earth, which shall be diverse from all kingdoms, and shall devour the whole earth, and shall tread it down, and break it in pieces. And the ten horns out of this kingdom are ten kings that shall arise: and another shall rise after them; and he shall be diverse from the first, and he shall subdue three kings. And he shall speak great words against the most

High, and shall wear out the saints of the most High, and think to change times and laws: and they shall be given into his hand until a time and times and the dividing of time. But the judgment shall sit, and they shall take away his dominion, to consume and to destroy it unto the end. And the kingdom and dominion, and the greatness of the kingdom under the whole heaven, shall be given to the people of the saints of the most High, whose kingdom is an everlasting kingdom, and all dominions shall serve and obey him (Daniel 7:23-27).

As in Daniel 2, this final earthly kingdom comes up after Greece (the third kingdom depicted); it's a terrible persecuting power (as was the power depicted by the iron in Daniel 2); and it extends to the end, when God establishes His kingdom (as does the last power in chapter 2). Also, just as the iron in the legs eventually changed to iron and clay (depicting perhaps a change in character of the kingdom even if the basic kingdom itself remains, for the iron stays until the end), a change occurs also with this last earthly power in Daniel 7. It starts out as a terrible beast until the emphasis shifts to the activity of the horn power (described as a "little horn" in verse 8, and as the "horn" in verse 1) that comes out of this beast but remains part of it. *The horn power, whatever it represents, is still part of the fourth beast; it's not a separate entity.* Thus, as in Daniel 2 in which the iron kingdom began after Greece and extended to the end of time (even though it was mixed with clay), the last beast in Daniel 7 comes up after Greece and goes to the end as well.

Another consideration: About four or five verses in Daniel 7 cover Babylon, Media-Persia, and Greece, which together span about four centuries. In contrast, the chapter uses about eleven verses to depict the activity of the fourth beast and the terrible little-horn power that is part of it. As with Daniel 2 and the iron in the statue, whatever this final power is, it's obviously something of great significance. This power, beginning after Greece, extends until the Lord sets up His kingdom; thus, it covers a period of at least two thousand years. The parallels between Daniel 2 and Daniel 7 are shown below in chart form:

| **Daniel 2** | **Daniel 7** |
|---|---|
| Babylon | Babylon |
| Media-Persia | Media-Persia |
| Greece | Greece |
| Final earthly kingdom | Final earthly kingdom |
| God's eternal kingdom | God's eternal kingdom |

Next, we come to the other parallel chapter, Daniel 8. As with Daniel 2 and Daniel 7, this chapter has the same sequence of Media-Persia, Greece, and then a final power, which—like the iron in Daniel 2 and the fourth beast in Daniel 7—is supernaturally destroyed. "[W]ithout hand" (verse 25) is how the chapter describes this power's demise.

The crucial question centers around the identity of that little-horn power in Daniel 8. What is it?

First (as shown above) Daniel 2 and Daniel 7 extend to "the time of the end" as we understand that phrase, that is, to the second coming of Christ and beyond. We saw, too, that when Daniel 8 talks about "the time of the end" (Daniel 8:17) or "the end" (verse 19), powerful evidence shows that it refers to the end in the same sense as do Daniel 2 and Daniel 7—the end of this present world. Thus, the horn power in Daniel 8, whatever it is, has to be something that comes down to "the end" or "the time of the end." Otherwise it's hard to make sense of those phrases about "the end" in Daniel 8, especially when viewed in the context of other chapters in Daniel (2, 7, 12), which without a doubt extend to the end of time.

Also, if one rejects this view of the end, what does one do with the parallels between Daniel 2 , 7, and 8? They can be summarized like this:

| Daniel 2 | Daniel 7 | Daniel 8 |
| --- | --- | --- |
| Babylon | Babylon | ____ |
| Media-Persia | Media-Persia | Media-Persia |
| Greece | Greece | Greece |
| Final kingdom in chapter | Final kingdom in chapter | Final kingdom in chapter |
| Supernatural destruction at end | Supernatural destruction at end | Supernatural destruction at end |

All three chapters proceed from Media-Persia, Greece, to the last kingdom depicted in each chapter before the supernatural intervention of God. In Daniel 2 and Daniel 7, it's unquestionable that this last kingdom in each chapter is the last earthly one before God's kingdom is established. Daniel 8, after the sequence of Media-Persia and Greece, has one more earthly power that is supernaturally destroyed by God. Whatever that final power is—which comes up after Greece and is supernaturally destroyed at "the end" (as were the two final kingdoms in Daniel 2 and Daniel 7)—the evidence powerfully suggests that this little horn power in Daniel 8 is the same power depicted in chapters 2 and 7. Given what we've seen so far (and from what's coming), the conclusion that the iron (and clay) kingdom in Daniel 2, the fourth beast (and little horn) of Daniel 7, and the little-horn of Daniel 8 are different depictions of the same power is inescapable.

We need to consider two more points about the horn power of Daniel 8 before we look at Brother Dale's identification, an identification that, if correct, would be our undoing as Seventh-day Adventists.

First, in volume one of the Daniel and Revelation Committee Series (a book that Brother Ratzlaff put in his bibliography) Dr. William Shea looked at the identity of this fourth beast; he focused particularly on the horn power in Daniel 7 and the horn power in Daniel 8. What Dr. Shea wrote is important because it helps show that whatever these powers represent, they appear to be the same entity:

> On the other hand, there are significant arguments in favor of identifying the little horns in these chapters [Daniel 7 and 8] as the same historical entity. First, the fact that the same symbol was used for both of them, whether in Aramaic (ch 7) or in Hebrew (ch 8) suggests at the outset that there could well be a connection between them. If a historical distinction had been intended there, the best way would have been to use a different symbol. But the symbol remained the same.
>
> Second, the powers represented by this same prophetic symbol both engage in similar actions; both appear and arise at a somewhat similar time in history; both begin small and become great (7:8 and 8:9); both are blasphemous powers (7:8, 25 and 8:11, 25); both persecute the saints of God (7:21, 25 and 8:11, 25); both appear to endure for protracted periods of prophetic time (7:25 and 8:14); and both eventually suffer similar fates (7:26 and 8:25).
>
> Thus when two powers represented by the same prophetic symbol arise and carry out the same kinds of actions in the same time slot in the flow of the visions, the probabilities appear to be on the side of those commentators who have identified them as the same historical entity. Some of the aspects of the work of the little horn in ch 7 are not mentioned in ch 8, and vice versa. The number of correspondences between them, however, is greater than those aspects of their work  not mentioned in both passages. None of these individual characteristics are mutually exclusive so as to rule out the possibility that they could refer to the same power.[5]

The second point deals with a specific description in Daniel 8 of the little horn. Two powers preceded the little horn in the vision—the ram (Daniel 8:3, 4) and the he-goat (verses 5-8), Media-Persia (verse 20) and Greece (verse 21) respectively. The ram was depicted as "great" (verse 4); the he-goat as "very great" (verse 8). In contrast to these two behemoths, the little-horn power was depicted as "exceeding great" (verse 9).

The Hebrew root word *gdl,* as a verb, is translated "great" in all three verses (KJV). In describing Media-Persia, the prophet used no modifier, only the verb *gdl.* Of course, that makes great sense, considering the size, scope, and longevity of the Medo-Persian Empire, which is dated (approximately) from 539 B.C. to about 331 B.C., about two centuries. At its apogee, Media-Persia covered more area than its Babylonian predecessor, or any previous empire. From Mt. Ararat in the north to Nubia in the south, from the Indus in the east to the Hellespont in the west, the Medo-Persian Empire, the ram of Daniel 8, certainly became "great."

The he-goat, or Greece, which followed, is depicted in the KJV as having "waxed very great" (Daniel 8:8). Here, the Hebrew verbal root *gdl* is modified by the words *ad meod, ad* being a common preposition meaning "as far as," "until," "up to" "unto," and so forth. *Meod* is a Hebrew word meaning "force," "abundance," "might," "exceedingly." It appears, for instance, in the famous verse, "And thou shalt love the Lord thy God with all thine heart, and with all thy soul, and with all thy *might* [from *meod*]." The phrase, *ad meod,* as it appears in Daniel 8:8, also appears elsewhere, such as in Genesis 27:33, "And Isaac trembled *very exceedingly"* (italics supplied).

The description, which makes Greece more *gdl* than Media-Persia aptly fits the historical record. The exploits of Greece, under the "notable horn between his eyes" (Alexander the Great) are legendary. The Greek Empire lasted (including the time of the four kings that followed Alexander) more than a century and a half approximately and covered an area greater than its two predecessors in the prophecy. It had everything Media-Persia had—and more. It was the most extensive empire that world had yet seen. No wonder, then, it is described as having "waxed very great" (verse 8), that is, greater than Media-Persia, which became only "great" (verse 4).

Now, in contrast to these two kingdoms, there's the final kingdom in Daniel 8, the little-horn power, the subject of our investigation. It is described in the KJV as having "waxed exceeding great" (verse 9) as opposed to Media-Persia ("great") and Greece ("very great").

Here, again, the verb is *gdl,* though modified with the adverb *ytr,* which comes from a root that means "to be left over" (sometimes used in the context of a "remnant"). In Daniel 8:9, in the form it appears, *ytr* can be translated "excellence," "excessive," "abundance," and "exceedingly." Does the word mean something even greater than *ad meod*, which modified *gdl* in reference to Greece? In other words, were the KJV translators justified, on purely linguistic grounds, in translating *ytr* with a word that seems to make it more intensive than the words applied to Greece? That is, while Greece waxes "very great" this last kingdom waxes "exceeding great," implying that however great Greece may have been, this last kingdom, the little horn, is even greater?

On linguistic grounds alone, the question can be argued either way. For our specific purpose, the question is irrelevant. You could argue that, contextually—given the much greater emphasis placed in Daniel 8 on the activity of the little horn (as opposed to either Media-Persia or Greece)—the KJV translators were justified in translating it in a manner that implies it was even greater than Greece. Nevertheless, we don't need to make such an argument because, whatever the differences between the two modifiers, one point is clear: This last kingdom (like the last kingdom in Daniel 2 and in Daniel 7) was greater than *Media-Persia*. Media-Persia is described as only "great," whereas the little-horn power is described as "exceedingly great." We don't need to rely on the linguistic debate between *ad meod* and *ytr.* The mere use of an adverb in verse 9, whatever it shows in relationship to Greece, clearly proves beyond the shadow of a doubt that this little-horn power is "greater" than the Medo-Persian Empire.

## THE "SLIVER"

Now, we left Brother Ratzlaff many pages ago with the first two kingdoms in Daniel 8, which he agreed with us were Media-Persia and Greece, respectively.[6] The key issue, again, deals with the identity of the "little horn" power in Daniel 8. Who is this horn power, the final earthly power to arise in this chapter, as well as in Daniel 2 and Daniel 7?

Let's first summarize, particularly in the context of the preceding prophetic chapters in Daniel.

1. The little horn, the final earthly power in Daniel 8, arises after Greece—as do the final earthly powers in Daniel 2 and Daniel 7.

2. This final earthly power, just like those in Daniel 2 and Daniel 7, is supernaturally destroyed at "the end," a phrase used in numerous ways in Daniel 8 and shown to mean the end of the world at the Second Coming and beyond.

3. Whatever this final earthly power is, in Daniel 2, Daniel 7, and Daniel 8, it arises after Greece and extends to the end of the world. Hence, the

power depicted in all three chapters must be in existence for many centuries. In fact, in all three chapters this power exists until the end, which means that it must be in existence even now because we are still between the fall of Greece and the second coming of Christ.

4. This final power in Daniel 8 is the same final power depicted in Daniel 2 and Daniel 7, a point made clear by this chart (shown above, but worth looking at again), which parallels the three chapters:

| **Daniel 2** | **Daniel 7** | **Daniel 8** |
|---|---|---|
| Babylon | Babylon | —— |
| Media-Persia | Media-Persia | Media-Persia |
| Greece | Greece | Greece |
| Final kingdom in chapter | Final kingdom in chapter | Final kingdom in chapter |
| Supernatural destruction at end | Supernatural destruction at end | Supernatural destruction at end |

As stated before, all three chapters follow a sequence from Media-Persia, Greece, to the last kingdom depicted in each chapter before the supernatural intervention of God. In Daniel 2 and Daniel 7, it's unquestionable that this last kingdom is the last earthly one before God's kingdom is established. Daniel 8, after the sequence of Media-Persia and Greece, has one more earthly power that is supernaturally destroyed by God. Whatever that final power is—which arises after Greece and is supernaturally destroyed at "the end" (as were the two final kingdoms in Daniel 2 and Daniel 7)—the evidence powerfully suggests that this little-horn power in Daniel 8 is the same power depicted in chapters 2 and 7.

5. This final earthly power in Daniel 8, as were the final earthly powers in chapters 2 and 7, is a persecuting power.

6. This final earthly power, as depicted in Daniel 2, 7, and 8, is in many ways more powerful than those kingdoms that preceded it—a point brought out by various traits, including the fact that in most cases, more verses and details are expended depicting it and its activities than are expended on the preceding powers.

Now, with these points regarding the little horn established, let's look at what Brother Dale has written. Who does he say this little horn is? Who do we say it is? Do we have enough information from the Bible and history to know who's right?

After writing about Media-Persia and Greece, and then quoting from Daniel 8:23-25 (the interpretation of the little horn given in the Bible itself) Brother Dale gives his answer to the question: Who is the little horn of Daniel 8?

> Nearly all Bible scholars believe the little horn to represent Antiochus Epiphanes IV. Daniel states that this power came from one of the divisions of Alexander's empire. It is clear that this is a wicked power, which did great havoc against the saints. Adventists make this little horn to be Rome. However, evidence that this has reference to Antiochus is overwhelming![7]

Our brother then goes on to "confront the 'sliver,' the teaching of the cleansing of the heavenly sanctuary and the investigative judgment, head on."[8] His point is simply this: If, indeed, the little horn is Antiochus Epiphanes IV, then the whole context of Daniel 8, far from extending to "the end"— that is, the end of the world—was fulfilled more than two thousand years ago, when this king defiled the temple in Jerusalem. If the little horn is Antiochus, the Adventist doctrine of the pre-Advent judgment, at least as understood from Daniel 8 (its foundation), is destroyed. The prophecy that we put in "the time of the end" (Daniel 8:17) or "the last end" or "the end" (Daniel 8:19) was, instead, consummated and completed more than a century before the death of Christ. If so, our whole teaching is rendered null and void. Our dear brother knows that, which is why he identifies the little horn as Antiochus.

In contrast, as Adventists, we (along with some of the early Reformers and various Protestants through history) believe that the little-horn power depicted in Daniel 8 (along with the fourth beast/horn of Daniel 7 and the iron/clay of Daniel 2) refers to Rome, that is—pagan and papal Rome, often depicted in the Bible as one power.

## COMPARING CHARACTERISTICS

Who is correct? All we need to do is to look at the characteristics of both Rome and Antiochus and see which (if either) fits. Because both these entities are quite different, the evidence should be conclusive.

After the death of Alexander the Great, the Grecian Empire (represented by the bronze in Daniel 2, the leopard in Daniel 7, and the he-goat in Daniel 8) separated into four kingdoms that existed in various stages until the Roman Empire ascended to political and military hegemony in the ancient world. One of those four kingdoms was the Seleucid, which ruled from what today is Syria. The entire Seleucid dynasty lasted from about 311 to 65 B.C.; more than twenty kings, at various times, sat on its throne. Among them was Antiochus IV Epiphanes, the subject of our discussion and, according to Brother Ratzlaff, the little-horn power of Daniel 8. Antiochus, not one of the Seleucids' more successful kings, was the eighth in line; about twelve Seleucid kings followed him.

In fact, Antiochus would hardly have been more than a historical footnote but for a three-year period of his eleven-year rule (175–164 B.C.) in which he defiled the sanctuary in Jerusalem after Palestine came under Seleucid rule in 198 B.C. In other words, Antiochus didn't conquer Palestine; he simply took over after it had already been subjugated. It was Antiochus's defiling of the sanctuary and its services, and this alone, that has caused many biblical commentators (including Brother Dale) to identify him as the power in Daniel that "magnified himself even to the prince of the host, and by him the daily sacrifice was taken away, and the place of his sanctuary was cast down. And an host was given him against the daily sacrifice by reason of transgression, and it cast down the truth to the ground; and it practised, and prospered" (Daniel 8:11, 12).

What did Antiochus do? Working in cahoots with Hellenizing Jews, Antiochus had a statue of Zeus built outside the temple at the altar of burnt offerings, on which unclean animals, more than likely pigs, were sacrificed. This defiling continued for about three years until the Jews, under the Maccabeans, regained control of the Temple Mount and re-established worship services according to the biblical pattern (hence, the cleansing of the sanctuary at the end of the 2,300 days in Daniel 8:14 is said to be a reference to this event). More details are given in the books of 1 and 2 Maccabees, apocryphal writings that never made it into the biblical canon.

Thus, the crucial question: Does Antiochus Epiphanes fit the description given of the little horn in Daniel 8? Remember, it's in this context, that of Antiochus in Daniel 8, that Dale Ratzlaff confronts the "sliver" in Adventist theology "head on." Let's look at the six characteristics of the little horn, listed above, and compare them with the reign of Antiochus.

1. The little horn, the final earthly power in Daniel 8, arises after Greece— as do the final earthly powers in Daniel 2 and Daniel 7.

Here, Antiochus fits—arising as he did amid the Seleucid dynasty, which came after the death of Alexander the Great and the disintegration of his empire.

2. This final earthly power, just like those in Daniel 2 and Daniel 7, is supernaturally destroyed at "the end," a phrase used in numerous ways in Daniel 8 and shown to mean the end of the world at the Second Coming and beyond.

With all due respect, Antiochus fails miserably here. A personage who died almost 200 years *before* Christ could hardly fulfill a prophecy that points to "the end." Also, there's no indication that Antiochus died by supernatural means.

3. Whatever this final earthly power is, in Daniel 2, Daniel 7, and Daniel 8, it arises after Greece and extends to the end of the world. Hence, the power depicted in all three chapters must be in existence for many centuries. In fact, in all three chapters this power exists until the end, which means that it must be in existence even now because we are still between the fall of Greece and the second coming of Christ.

Again, a king who perished (along with the whole dynasty that he temporarily ruled) in the second century B.C. hardly fits the entity depicted in Daniel 8, which arises after Greece and extends all the way to "the end" of the world.

4. This final power in Daniel 8 is the same final power depicted in Daniel 2 and Daniel 7. All three chapters follow a sequence from Media-Persia, Greece, to the last kingdom depicted in each chapter before the supernatural intervention of God. In Daniel 2 and Daniel 7, it's unquestionable that this last kingdom is the last earthly one before God's kingdom is established. Daniel 8, after the sequence of Media-Persia and Greece, has one more earthly power that is supernaturally destroyed by God. Whatever that final power is—which arises after Greece and is supernaturally destroyed at "the end" (as were the two final kingdoms in Daniel 2 and Daniel 7)—the evidence powerfully suggests that this little-horn power in Daniel 8 is the same power depicted in chapters 2 and 7. (See also the chart above on page 38.)

Again, with these clear parallels between Daniel 2, 7, and 8, Antiochus is utterly disqualified. How could Antiochus be the last kingdom which exists before God establishes His kingdom at the end of the age—when he vanished in the second century B.C.? The answer, of course, is that he can't be.

5. This final earthly power in Daniel 8, as were the final earthly powers in chapters 2 and 7, is a persecuting power.

Antiochus *was* a persecuting power, so in this manner, he does fit this characteristic.

6. This final earthly power, as depicted in Daniel 2, 7, and 8, is in many ways more powerful than those kingdoms that preceded it—a point

brought out by various traits, including the fact that in most cases, more verses and details are expended depicting it and its activities than are expended on the preceding powers.

Here, too, Antiochus isn't even close. As one not-entirely-successful king in a dynasty that was, at its best, weaker and smaller than either Greece or Media-Persia, Antiochus, even at the height of his power, doesn't fit this attribute of the little horn, which beyond doubt is depicted as greater than Media-Persia and, arguably, greater than Greece. Again, Antiochus's only claim to historical infamy is the three-year period in which he defiled the Jerusalem temple, an activity that hardly merits the time, space, and verbiage the Bible expends in describing the little-horn power.

Of the six characteristics of the little horn, we've seen that Antiochus fulfilled two: He arose after Greece, and he was a persecuting power. The remaining four characteristics—that he be supernaturally destroyed at the end of the world, that he exist for many centuries, even up through today and beyond, that he be the last earthly kingdom before God establishes His final kingdom, and that he be greater than the kingdoms which preceded him (especially Media-Persia)—unquestionably disqualify him from fulfilling the role of the little horn.

Of the two characteristics he does fit—a power that comes up after Greece, and a persecuting power—neither, either alone or together, makes a positive identification. In contrast, one power fits not only the two characteristics that Antiochus fits, but all others as well—and that power is Rome, pagan and papal.

1. The little horn arises after Greece. Rome fits.

2. The little horn will be destroyed supernaturally at the end. Of course, that's still future. However, for a power to be supernaturally destroyed at the end, it, at least, has to exist to the end. After 1,500 years, Rome (now in the papal stage) is still going strong and shows no indication of disappearing any time soon. Rome certainly has the potential of fulfilling this characteristic, unlike Antiochus which has no potential at all in fulfilling it.

3. The little horn, coming up after Greece, has to exist for many centuries, even into our time. Rome, arising after Greece and continuing even into our time, fits perfectly.

4. In Daniel 2, the power after Greece is Rome, the last power before God's final kingdom. In Daniel 7, the power after Greece is Rome, the last power before God's final kingdom. And in Daniel 8, the power after Greece—the last power—must be Rome as well.

5. Rome was a persecuting power.

6. The little-horn power is greater than the powers that preceded it—an attribute that, again, Rome (both pagan and papal) alone fits.

There is no question that on this point—the identity of the little-horn power of Daniel—one can be as dogmatic as dogmatic can be: That power is solely, totally, and only Rome, pagan and papal. What other power arose after Greece and is still in existence today, especially in the context in which it appears in Daniel 8, that of a power intricately involved with God's church? Faith is needed to believe in the Second Coming, in the resurrection of the dead, and in a millennium in heaven. But who needs faith to believe that Rome is the power that fulfills this prophecy, especially when history sets it out so clearly and unambiguously?

Look at chapter 8, as a whole, especially in parallel with chapters 2 and 7, all of which make Rome, not Antiochus Epiphanes, the final power that arises before the end of the world. Let's look at it again in chart form:

| Daniel 2 | Daniel 7 | Daniel 8 |
|---|---|---|
| Babylon | Babylon | —— |
| Media-Persia | Media-Persia | Media-Persia |
| Greece | Greece | Greece |
| Rome (pagan/papal) | Rome (pagan/papal) | Rome (pagan/papal) |
| Supernatural destruction at end | Supernatural destruction at end | Supernatural destruction at end |

Replace "Rome (pagan/papal)" with "Antiochus" in each slot, and you'll see how untenable the Antiochus interpretation is.

The Adventist position regarding Rome as the little horn is as firm as world history itself. No matter how politically incorrect this view, we can't waffle here. Fortunately, we don't need to.

## "A FEW, CLEAR BIBLE REFERENCES"

Now, does this argument itself prove the validity of the Adventist teaching on the pre-Advent judgment? Of course not. It wasn't intended to. The intention, rather, was to examine some of the "few, clear Bible references" that, according to Brother Dale, nullify the pre-Advent judgment, among them these verses in Daniel 8, which supposedly prove (the evidence, Brother Dale says, is "overwhelming") that the little-horn power is Antiochus Epiphanes, not Rome. The evidence is, indeed, "overwhelming," and it refutes our brother's position.

Much more work has debunked the Antiochus interpretation, no matter how popular and common it remains. And this leads to a disturbing aspect of Brother Dale's book—something mentioned earlier but worth repeating. In *Selected Studies on Prophetic Interpretation,* in a chapter titled, "Why Antiochus IV Is Not the Little Horn of Daniel 8," Adventist scholar William Shea wrote more than thirty pages showing, point by point, the inadequacy of the Antiochus interpretation. Brother Dale claims that Daniel 8 depicts "the persecutions of Antiochus with such exact detail,"[9] that some liberal scholars are convinced it had been written after the historical events surrounding Antiochus had already occurred, an amazing claim, especially in light of all the work done to show just how Antiochus does not, and cannot, fit the prophecy. And, for some reason, Brother Ratzlaff makes no attempt to counter any of the arguments that Dr. Shea used to decimate the Antiochus interpretation. To claim that he just didn't know about Dr. Shea's work doesn't work because he listed *Selected Studies on Prophetic Interpretation* in his book *CDSDA.* In other words, Brother Dale knew about Shea's book but chose not to deal with the arguments in it, a tactic taken even by many scholars within the church as well.

Why would someone attempting to debunk a key teaching of a church ignore the church's best defense of that teaching? One can only speculate. But rather than deal with our defenses, Brother Dale acts as if they weren't there and, instead, makes sweeping, broad statements that prove paltry upon the most cursory examination. Again, for a ministry that aspires to become "the source for accurate information on Adventist doctrine and practice for the Evangelical world,"[10] this lapse is telling.

It's not the only one, either.

---

[1] For a detailed study on the relationship of these chapters, see *Symposium on Daniel* (Biblical Research Institute, Silver Spring, MD) "Unity of Daniel," William Shea, pp. 165–220. Daniel and Revelation Committee Series, vol 2. 1986.

[2] *CDSDA,* pp. 165, 166.

[3] *Ibid.,* p. 167.

[4] *Ibid.,* p. 168.

[5] William Shea, *Selected Studies on Prophetic Interpretation,* Daniel and Revelation Committee Series, vol. 1 (General Conference of Seventh-day Adventists, 1982), "Why Antiochus IV Is Not the Little Horn of Daniel 8," pp. 30, 31.

[6] *CDSDA,* p. 167.

[7] *Ibid.,* pp. 167, 168.

[8] *Ibid, p.168.*

[9] *Ibid.*

[10] Taken from *www.LifeAssuranceMinistries.com* (January 26, 2001).

# CHAPTER FOUR

# FROM
# ANTIQUITY
## TO ETERNITY

To recap: Dale Ratzlaff, a former Adventist minister, writes a 380-page book that denounces the pre-Advent judgment as "cultic," even though only one chapter (about fifteen pages) in his entire tome deals *specifically* with biblical texts regarding the doctrine of the judgment itself. The rest of the work, though touching on the judgment doctrine at various places, attacks Ellen White, William Miller, the Seventh-day Adventist Church, and so forth. This point should not be overlooked for it says much more than Mr. Ratzlaff ever intended.

Nevertheless, we'll continue (for now) to examine the "few, clear Bible references" that Brother Dale claims, "are more than enough to show, beyond the shadow of a doubt, that the doctrine of the cleansing of the heavenly sanctuary and the investigative judgment is not supported by Scripture and is contrary to it at almost every point."[1] We've already delved into the first of those references, those in Daniel 8 that, according to Brother Ratzlaff, refer to Antiochus Epiphanes and therefore could have nothing to do with a pre-Advent judgment that occurs in the last days. That position, we have shown, is untenable. I propose to show that most of his other biblical arguments aren't any better than the ones we have already examined—and that some are worse. Before looking at Brother Dale's other arguments against the judgment, I want to summarize (and, in some cases, elaborate on) a few points and, then, respond to his specific arguments.

## DANIEL 2

Let's begin with Daniel 2. Starting with Babylon and ending with Christ's eternal kingdom, Daniel 2 forms the prophetic basis of the entire book of Daniel. In one way or another, most of the prophecies that follow elaborate on what is set out in this chapter. Chapter 2 itself could be broadly summarized like this:

Babylon
Media-Persia
Greece
Rome
Second coming of Jesus

I can't stress enough how important Daniel 2 is to our prophetic interpretation. (Study the chapter itself as you read what I write here). Daniel 2 establishes a foundation for our views that are as firm, literally, as world history itself. It lays down the entire prophetic parameters of Daniel. It contains the method for how we should interpret these prophecies, and it proves that these prophecies begin in antiquity and follow a continuous sweep of world history that extends to "the time of the end," that is, beyond our day and into the future world of God's eternal kingdom. This last point can't be overemphasized, especially in light of various theories about the interpretation of Daniel's prophecies.

Daniel 2—giving a clear, unbroken succession of kingdoms, starting with Babylon and ending when this present world does—reveals the need for the historicist approach to interpreting these prophecies. The chapter shows that these prophecies are based *in history*, in a progression of history that starts in antiquity and climaxes in the future.

Study Daniel 2:37-44 where Daniel specifically says that the prophecy is about four great world empires that begin with Nebuchadnezzar's Babylon and end when the God of heaven sets up His own eternal kingdom. These verses, then, contain the key to understanding the prophecies because *they themselves interpret the prophecies,* proving that the historicist approach to interpretation (which Adventists stand almost alone in still adhering to) is what the text demands. Historicism teaches what Daniel 2 teaches—that these prophecies follow the sweep of human history from antiquity to eternity and that they are not focused solely on events in the far past or solely on events in the future, but cover the scope of world history. Thus, right out of the gate, in the first prophetic section of Daniel, we are given the key to understand its prophecies.

Daniel 2, then, denudes the argument that all these prophecies were fulfilled in the distant past, such as during the reign of Antiochus Epiphanes, as some claim. Daniel 2 interprets the final part of the vision—the stone that is cut out without hands and that totally annihilates all the previous world kingdoms until they become like chaff and the wind carries them away, and "no place was found for them" (verse 35)—like this: "And in the days of these kings shall the God of heaven set up a kingdom, which shall never be destroyed: and the kingdom shall not be left to other people, but it shall break in pieces and consume all these kingdoms, and it shall stand for ever" (Daniel 2:44). This is the end of the present world as we know it—an event still in the future. Daniel's interpretation, which begins in Babylon and ends in the future, utterly destroys any interpretation that limits the apocalyptic prophecies of his book to the distant past.

Daniel 2 also nullifies attempts to place all these events in the future alone, and to interpret the symbols as present or upcoming entities that will engage in massive apocalyptic battles before the end of the world. Daniel 2:37, in which the prophet names Babylon itself (personified by Nebuchadnezzar) as the first part of the statue, proves that at least the beginning symbol of the prophecy deals with events hundreds of years before Christ, not just with future kingdoms *alone* (usually centered in or around the Middle East). We don't have to guess or speculate. The interpretation, and the method of interpretation, is given—not just for Daniel 2, but also for chapters 7 and 8, both of which are elaborations and reiterations of what is in Daniel 2. In fact, the internal evidence in both chapters 7 and 8 alone (even much more so when paralleled with each other and with Daniel 2) demands the historicist interpretation because that's how these prophecies interpret themselves—as a depictions of great world empires, the first rising in antiquity, and the last ending when God establishes His final kingdom.

Finally, Daniel 2 voids the arguments of those who give it (and chapters 7 and 8) multiple interpretations, claiming that in one era it meant one thing, and that in another it means something else, and that in our time it means something different. What gives anyone the license to give multiple fulfillments to the chapter, especially when Daniel himself says what the prophecy is about—four great kingdoms that will arise until God's final kingdom comes and is established (Daniel 2:37-44)? Daniel doesn't say that these prophecies mean one thing in one era, another thing in another, and something else at another time, and that all of these approaches are valid. He says, without obfuscation, what the prophecy covers—a series of world empires that climax at the end of the world at the Second Coming. The prophecies, which interpret themselves, give themselves an interpretation that's anchored in the outline of world history, a massive unmovable bulk that by nature isn't amenable to the notion of multiple fulfillments and interpretations.

By naming Babylon itself as the head of gold (verse 38), Daniel 2 firmly nails the prophecy down to earth, to a specific world kingdom. This fact alone denudes the multiple fulfillment paradigm. If Babylon is all but named, what justification do we have to allow the other symbols in the prophecy to be given different interpretations in different times? Can we just leave Babylon the same in each reinterpretation, while changing every other symbol in the prophecy to fit whatever interpretation happens to be in vogue? Or can we just ignore the unambiguous identification of Babylon given in the chapter—that is, the Babylon of Nebuchadnezzar which existed many centuries before Christ, thus firmly rooting the prophecy in history—and come up with some other method of interpretation that applies the other symbols in the prophecy to another era? Daniel 2 sets down parameters that don't leave many options on how to interpret it or the other apocalyptic prophecies in the same book.

The case against multiple fulfillment is made even stronger when we look at Daniel chapters 2, 7, and 8 together. As we've seen (and will see again), these chapters basically deal with five major kingdoms—four earthly and one divine. Of the five, four are specifically named. The five empires, or kingdoms, could be expressed like this:

Babylon (Daniel 2:38)
Media-Persia (Daniel 8:20)
Greece (Daniel 8:21)
(Unnamed fourth kingdom)
God's eternal kingdom (Daniel 2:44; 7:14, 18, 27)

So, from within the prophecies themselves, four out of the five elements are named by the Lord. And considering what's named—massive empires immovably and immutably rooted in world history itself—the idea that we can somehow give these prophecies different fulfillments in different eras certainly doesn't arise from anything inherent in the texts themselves.

## THE LITTLE HORN OF DANIEL 7

Daniel 7 gives us basically the same prophetic sequence (with the same historicist hermeneutic built right in) as Daniel 2—only with more detail. Again, I highly recommend that you follow this train of thought in the Bible itself. (My book, *1844 Made Simple* could help too.)

In chapter 7, Daniel has a dream of four beasts that arise from the great sea. These beasts are depicted as great kingdoms that arise one after the other (just as the vision showed in Daniel 2) followed by the establishment of God's kingdom (Daniel 7:1-18). A succession of world powers? A sweep of world history? *Again, the prophecy itself teaches us how to interpret it, and teaches us to use the historicist method, nothing else.* Throughout history, many commentators have depicted these beasts, and rightly so, as Babylon, Media-Persia, Greece, Rome, and God's eternal kingdom, just as they have done with Daniel 2. This interpretation is not uniquely Adventist, not by a long shot.

A great deal of detail, however, is given to the fourth beast in chapter 7. (Daniel sought "to know the truth of the fourth beast" [verse 19]), the power that arises right after Greece.

What great empire came up after the demise of Greece? None other than pagan Rome, the power that actually brought about the downfall of Greece. How could the fourth beast symbolize anything other than Rome, a massive world power, a persecuting, devouring power (Daniel 7:7) that, again, comes up right after the fall of the power that preceded it? Not many other candidates fit, and certainly not in this context. It can be only pagan Rome, which is how it has been identified by commentators for centuries. For us, from our perspective of looking back into the historical record, this identification doesn't require much faith. Who needs faith to believe that pagan Rome arose after the demise of Greece? It's like saying, *"I have faith that Napoleon was routed at Waterloo."*

Now, out of this fourth beast, pagan Rome, comes a terrible little-horn power which has many qualities similar to the little horn of Daniel 8. Here's the crucial point worth repeating: This horn power in Daniel 7 is not a separate beast but a part of the fourth beast, pagan Rome. In other words, unlike all the previous beasts, which were completely separate beasts representing completely separate powers, this little horn is not separate from Rome. It is part of Rome, simply representing a later phase of it.

The prophecy is an accurate prediction of what happened with pagan Rome. Was Rome eventually replaced by an entirely new kingdom as were the previous kingdoms, all depicted by new, different beasts? Or did Rome change into something else, an extension of what it was, just as in Daniel 2 the iron, representing the fourth kingdom, extends all the way to the feet and the toes of the statute, showing that even in chapter 2 the fourth kingdom remains to the end, even if in another form?

Of course, the correct answer is the latter. The fourth beast never left; it just changed, that's all. Some historians don't even like talking about the "fall" of pagan Rome; instead they prefer to see it as a transformation (it's not called the *Roman* Catholic Church for nothing). Again, the point can't be stressed enough: The little-horn power is part of the fourth beast. It's not a new power, as were each of the three preceding empires. As one of the greatest political philosophers wrote in one of the greatest political treatises: "If a man consider the origin of this great ecclesiastical dominion, he will easily perceive that the papacy is no other than the ghost of the deceased Roman Empire, sitting crowned on the grave thereof."[2]

Look at how the little-horn power is depicted in the vision itself. After describing the first three beasts (Babylon, Media-Persia, and Greece, all of which, as we've seen, have been named by Daniel (even if under different symbols) in various parts of his book, Daniel says:

> After this I saw in the night visions, and behold a *fourth beast, dreadful and terrible, and strong exceedingly; and it had great iron teeth: it devoured and brake in pieces, and stamped the residue with the feet of it: and it was diverse from all the beasts that were before it; and it had ten horns. I considered the horns, and, behold, there came up among them another little horn, before whom there were three of the first horns plucked up by the roots: and, behold, in this horn were eyes like the eyes of a man, and a mouth speaking great things. I beheld till the thrones were cast down, and the Ancient of days did sit, whose garment was white as snow, and the hair of his head like the pure wool: his throne was like the fiery flame, and his wheels as burning fire. A fiery stream issued and came forth from before him: thousand thousands ministered unto him, and ten thousand times ten thousand stood before him: the judgment was set, and the books were opened. . . .* **And there was given him dominion, and glory, and a kingdom, which shall not be destroyed** (Daniel 7:7-10, 14, emphasis supplied).

Read these verses over and over until the clear, undeniable sequence of events becomes locked in your mind. After Babylon, Media-Persia, and Greece, comes a fourth power (pagan Rome), and out of the fourth power comes a little horn (still a part of the fourth beast), followed by a judgment in heaven— a judgment that (as we will see) leads to the establishment of God's kingdom.

The sheer broad sweep of what happens makes the identity undeniable. After Greece this fourth power arises that extends (as we saw previously) to the end of world. That fourth power, the power that brought down the third one, is Rome. And just as the fourth power had two phases— the first focusing on the beast itself, and the second on the little horn that comes out of the fourth beast—so, too, Rome had two phases, a pagan phase that brought about the demise of Greece, and a papal phase that extends to the time of the end.

Daniel 7, then, could be summarized like this:

> Babylon
> Media-Persia
> Greece
> Rome (pagan/papal)
> Judgment in heaven
> Second Coming

Study Daniel 7 until you can see that sequence; it's crucial. As I stressed in *1844 Made Simple*, this specific sequence—little horn, judgment scene in heaven, Second Coming—appears three times in Daniel 7, emphasizing its significance. We've already looked at one depiction (Daniel 7:7-10); let's look at the two others:

> Then I would know the truth of *the fourth beast,* which was diverse from all the others, exceeding dreadful, whose teeth were of iron, and his nails of brass; which devoured, brake in pieces, and stamped the residue with his feet; And of the ten horns that were in his head, and of the other which came up, and before whom three fell; even of that horn that had eyes, and a mouth that spake very great things, whose look was more stout than his fellows. I beheld, and the same horn made war with the saints, and prevailed against them; *Until the Ancient of days came, and judgment was given to the saints of the most High;* **and the time came that the saints possessed the kingdom** (Daniel 7:19-22, emphasis supplied).

Again, notice the sequence—fourth beast (which includes the little horn), *judgment in heaven,* God's kingdom. Here it is again:

Thus he said, The *fourth beast* shall be the fourth kingdom upon earth, which shall be diverse from all kingdoms, and shall devour the whole earth, and shall tread it down, and break it in pieces. And the ten horns out of this kingdom are ten kings that shall arise: and another shall arise after them; and he shall be diverse from the first, and he shall subdue three kings. And he shall speak great words against the most High, and shall wear out the saints of the most High, and think to change times and laws: and they shall be given into his hand until a time and times and the dividing of time. *But the judgment shall sit,* **and they shall take away his dominion, to consume and to destroy it unto the end. And the kingdom and dominion, and the greatness of the kingdom under the whole heaven, shall be given to the people of the saints of the most High, whose kingdom is an everlasting kingdom, and all dominions shall serve and obey him** (Daniel 7:23-27, emphasis supplied).

How could the sequence be any clearer or more concrete?

### Little horn
### *Judgment in heaven*
### God's eternal kingdom

I'm not going into the powerful evidence, revealed in the description of the little horn, that make papal Rome the *only* plausible interpretation. I deal with that in my book *1844 Made Simple.* Both volumes 1 and 2 of the Daniel and Revelation Committee Series explore the evidence in detail. Suffice it to say that a power which arises directly out of pagan Rome (Daniel 7:8, 20, 24), a blasphemous and religious power (Daniel 7:8, 20, 25), a persecuting power (Daniel 7:21, 25), and a power that will think "to change times and laws" (Daniel 7:25) doesn't leave many options, especially because a lot of detail is presented about this little horn (more so than about Babylon, Media-Persia, Greece, or pagan Rome), which means it's obviously a major player in world history, on a par with the empires that preceded it. How many persecuting powers that rose directly out of pagan Rome became a massive world empire with overt religious overtones? The options are limited. In fact, with one more detail, the identity is unmistakable.

It's in the description of the little-horn power that the first apocalyptic time prophecy in Daniel appears. According to Daniel 7:25, the saints will "be given into his [that is, the little horn's] hand until a time and times and the dividing of time." This period is almost universally recognized by Bible scholars (not just Adventist scholars) to mean three-and-a-half years. As one example, the *King James Study Bible* by Thomas Nelson (not an Adventist publication), interprets Daniel 7:25 like this:

> A time and times and the dividing of time (or "a times and times and half a time") is an expression used in Daniel and in Revelation to refer to three-and-a-half years, or 1,260 days, or 42 months (12:7; Rev. 11:2; 12:6, 14; 13:5).

Thus even non-Seventh-day Adventists don't have a problem turning the "times, time, and half a time" into 1,260 days. All one needs to do, next, is to apply the day-year principle to the 1,260 days, and it becomes 1,260 years.

Of course, Brother Dale attacks the day-year principle, ignoring Dr. Shea's two chapters in Volume 1 of the Daniel and Revelation Committee Series, which prove not only the validity of the day-year principle *in toto* but why it must be applied to this prophecy in particular. I will address the issue of the day-year principle later. Suffice it to say this much: The little-horn power arises directly out of pagan Rome, which met its demise (as *pagan* Rome) about the fifth or sixth century A.D. Out of it arises this little-horn power, which persecutes the saints for 1,260 "days" (Daniel 7:23-25). After this persecution comes a judgment in heaven that leads to the establishment of God's final kingdom (verses 26, 27).

Now, either the time frame is literal (three and one-half actual years) or it's prophetic (1,260 actual years). Which option works best?

Amid all the prophetic symbols of Daniel 7 (winged lions and leopards, a beast with iron teeth, a horn that has eyes and a mouth), we find a time prophecy depicting the activity of a horn that has a mouth and eyes. If one takes the time frame as a literal three and one-half years (even though it appears amid all these symbols), then one of two options are possible.

First, the persecution was put on hold for at least 1,500 years—remember, the little horn arises after the demise of pagan Rome, which is fifth to sixth century A.D. Meanwhile, the judgment that follows the 1,260 days of persecution ends with the second coming of Christ, which is now at least into the twenty-first century. A major gap, therefore, must exist between the time the little horn arises (sixth century A.D.) and the 1,260 days of persecution that come right before the final judgment, which leads to the Second Coming. Under this scenario, a persecuting power arises out of pagan Rome, *but that persecution doesn't begin for at least 1,500 years and counting?* Remember, we're already in the twenty-first century, and God's kingdom isn't here yet, and it arises after the literal 1,260 days of persecution. That position is possible, but it's not plausible. Besides, nothing in the text indicates that this persecution is put off until the end; all the characteristics of the little horn appear to apply it in total.

The other option is that because these characteristics seem to apply in total to the little horn, with no indication of a delay, then the three and one-half years of persecution should have started early in the little horn's career. This means they must have ended about 1,500 years ago, around the fifth to sixth centuries A.D., 1,260 days after they started. If so, then the judgment that follows has been in session for almost a millennium and a half. This position is likewise possible, but rather untenable, especially for those who mock the Adventist view of the 1844 judgment, saying it's silly for a judgment to be going on for so long, that is, since 1844.

In short, a literal interpretation of Daniel 7:25, which makes the persecution by the little-horn power only three and one-half literal years, is improbable to the point of nonsense.

In contrast, if the time frame is prophetic (as are the symbols that surround it) and the day-year principle is applied, then the prophecy sweeps across history, going from the fifth to sixth centuries A.D. and ending up somewhere in the late eighteenth or early nineteenth century, bringing it down much closer to the "time of the end," as do all these other prophecies (Daniel 2; 7; and 8). Maybe for this reason, along with others, Bible expositors for centuries, even before the existence of the Seventh-day Adventist Church, used the day-year principle for Daniel 7:25. It's not an exclusive Adventist interpretation, even if we are almost alone now in clinging to it.

So, regarding the little horn, we have a religious power, a *Roman* power, a persecuting power, a power that arises directly out of pagan Rome, a power that extends across a span of time covering at least 1,260 years. Who could it be? Antiochus Epiphanes? Please! Islam? A nice try but, first, Islam didn't arise directly out of pagan Rome, and second, it's hardly a Roman power.

What else is there other than papal Rome? It fits perfectly. Though the older I get, the less dogmatic I am about almost everything, the identity

of the little horn as papal Rome is something one can afford to be obnox-
iously dogmatic about.

Thus, if one begins the 1,260 years in the sixth century, the beginning of
papal hegemony, then the 1,260 years end somewhere in the late eighteenth
or early nineteenth century. However applicable the dates of 538–1798
A.D. may be, and whatever evidence justifies those dates, we don't need
them. Instead, with two all-but-irrefutable points, i.e., the little horn as
papal Rome and the application of the day-year principle to the "time,
times and the dividing of time" of Daniel 7:25, we can show that the
judgment scene in heaven, which occurs after the 1,260-year period, is an
event that happens sometime after the late eighteenth or early nineteenth
century, and before the Second Coming. In fact, the texts show, irrefut-
ably, that this judgment is what leads to the Second Coming.

Here's Daniel 7 again, this time looking at it with Daniel's first apocalyptic time prophecy imbedded in the sequence. What we've added, too,
are the approximate times that each of the preceding empires collapsed.
Though historians often put specific dates on these events, centering
around decisive military battles, the collapse of one empire and the rise of
another usually occurs over many years, not just one:

Babylon
(Ends early to mid-sixth century B.C.)

Media-Persia
(From early to mid-sixth century to early to mid-fourth century B.C)

Greece
(From early to mid-fourth century to mid-second century B.C.)

Pagan Rome
(From mid-second century B.C. to fifth-sixth century A.D.)

Papal Rome
(Persecution from sixth century A.D. to eighteenth-nineteenth century
A.D.)

Judgment in heaven

Second Coming

Sure, the papacy didn't end in the late eighteenth or early nineteenth century, but that's not what the prophecy says. Instead, it says only that persecution would last for this length of time, or at least that phase of that persecution (Revelation 13, of course, talks about a resurgence of papal persecution, but that's another issue).

Thus, what's clear, so far, from Daniel 7 is a massive judgment scene in heaven, a judgment that occurs sometime *after* the 1,260 years of papal persecution, sometime after the *late* eighteenth or early nineteenth century, and that leads to the establishment of God's kingdom.

## NOT MENTIONED BY NAME?

One question, however, that has arisen is: Why, between the prophecies of Daniel 2, 7, and 8, are all of the kingdoms named except the fourth one, Rome? How much easier it would be, and how much futile and false speculation would have been saved, had the prophecy simply named the fourth kingdom as were Babylon, Media-Persia, Greece, and God's final kingdom. On the other hand, the naming of the others still hasn't stopped all manner of prognostications and interpretations that identify these powers as everything but what the text itself says they are. Some claim that Rome wasn't named because Daniel's book is not prophetic and that he didn't write during the Babylonian and early Medo-Persian Empire, as he says he did. Daniel, they argue, lived during the Grecian Empire and simply recounted history that already happened—rather than predicting events before they occurred. In other words, the accounts of the lions' den, the fiery furnace, the command to kill the wise men, the dreams and visions—all this was made up, fables that have no historical authenticity whatsoever. This view is pandemic among Bible scholars, including (unfortunately) some of our own. It's particularly popular among those who hold the Antiochus interpretation of the little horn.

A major problem with that concept (and there are many others, to be sure) is that even if one does accept the later date of Daniel (pure speculation, actually), which puts the authorship of the book around the middle of the second century B.C., Daniel still did an amazing job describing the rise of the pagan Roman Empire and its disintegration into the different nation-states of Europe more than five hundred years later (Daniel 2:41-44). There are also Daniel's predictions regarding the transformation of pagan Rome into papal Rome in the fifth to sixth century A.D. (Daniel 7:23-25), not bad for a guy who was, supposedly, writing about a century and a half before Christ (it would be like someone a century before Luther depicting the rise and fall of the Soviet empire).

Instead, maybe Rome isn't directly named because the Lord knew that Rome would be in sole control of the Scriptures for centuries, and had the leaders seen the empire distinctly named, *particularly in such a bad light,* they could have destroyed the Scriptures or the book of Daniel or at least the implicated chapters. As it was, not sure what the texts were talking about, Rome could give it identities other than itself. Meanwhile, the Lord kept that identity hidden, knowing that He would, at the right time, raise up people, particularly the Protestant Reformers, who would discover the true identity of that little-horn power. After all, Daniel does say that his words would be "closed up and sealed till the time of the end" (Daniel 12:9).

In fact, Jews who lived during the Roman Empire would often interpret these same prophecies like this: Babylon, Media-Persia, Greece, and— Edom. Why Edom? Because, afraid of the Romans, the Jews hid the interpretation, something that the Lord in His divine providence and foresight did hundreds of years earlier in Daniel itself.

At the same time, although the Lord didn't name Rome in the prophecy (however obvious the identification), He did so in the New Testament, where Rome is the crucial background player. The New Testament itself— which takes place during the kingdom that arose after Greece (that is, the fourth kingdom of Daniel 2 and 7, the third one in Daniel 8)—is filled with reference after reference to Rome or Roman power (in this case, the pagan phase of Rome). The Gospels, the book of Acts, the Epistles, all unfold in a Roman environment. Daniel mentions by name Babylon, Media-Persia, and Greece, while the New Testament names Rome, the power that arises after Greece and dominates the world during the time of Christ and afterward.

Many texts in the New Testament, either directly or indirectly, point to Rome and Rome's power: "And it came to pass in those days, that there went out a decree from Caesar Augustus, that *all the world* should be taxed" (Luke 2:1, italics supplied). Notice "all the world" should be taxed. Only a world power could tax all the world. Daniel 7:23 says that the fourth beast will "devour the whole earth," and—according to this text in Luke—it was Caesar who issued the decree. Who, or what, could be more of an apt symbol of Rome? (See also John 11:48; Matthew 22:17; Luke 3:1; Acts 25:21.)

Also Jesus, talking about the future destruction of Jerusalem, said: "And when ye shall see Jerusalem compassed with armies, then know that the desolation thereof is nigh. Then let them which are in Judaea flee to the mountains; and let them which are in the midst of it depart out; and let not them that are in the countries enter there into" (Luke 21:20, 21). In the parallel passage, in Matthew, Jesus says, "When ye therefore shall see the abomination of desolation, spoken of by Daniel the prophet, stand in the holy place, (whoso readeth, let him understand:) Then let them which be in Judaea flee into the mountains" (Matthew 24:15).

Thus, in the context of the destruction of Jerusalem, *by the Romans*, (one would be hard pressed to find a serious scholar who doesn't believe that Jesus is not referring here to the Roman destruction of Jerusalem in A.D. 70) Jesus linked the Roman Empire to the book of Daniel. Jesus, therefore, not only points to Rome, but places it within Daniel itself, where three times phrasing linked to "the abomination of desolation" spoken of by Jesus, in reference to Daniel, is found. They are Daniel 9:27; Daniel 11:31; Daniel 12:11. Of particular interest is its use in Daniel 9:24-27, a prophecy that most scholars see pointing to, among other things, the destruction of Jerusalem by Rome, a prophecy that (as we'll see) is tied directly to both Daniel 7 and Daniel 8.

The point is this: Daniel doesn't come right out and name Rome because the New Testament all but does it for us. Thus, following the Protestant formula of the Bible being its own interpreter, we find all four empires depicted in Daniel named in the Bible.

## THE LITTLE HORN AND THE JUDGMENT

Thus Daniel 7 powerfully presents the foundation of the pre-Advent judgment. Study the clear sequence of events: Babylon, after Babylon, Media-Persia; after Media-Persia, Greece; after Greece, pagan Rome; after pagan Rome, papal Rome (for 1,260 years); after papal Rome (the 1,260-year phase), judgment in heaven that leads to the Second Coming. Focus on the solid, immovable train of events—empire after empire after empire followed by a heavenly judgment—that leads to the Second Coming. This heavenly judgment, the pre-Advent judgment, is as firmly rooted as the massive world empires that pave the way toward it. We're on unshakable ground with this prophecy. We must learn it until it becomes second nature; then we'll be able to withstand almost any attack on our prophetic foundation. Daniel 7 stands as an in-your-face proof of the pre-Advent judgment, an event of clearly colossal importance because it leads to the Second Coming and the establishment of God's eternal kingdom.

Now, some (including Brother Dale) seek to debunk this interpretation of the judgment in Daniel 7, arguing that the judgment is against the little-horn power alone, not some final pre-Advent judgment that involves God's people. In other words, this judgment has nothing to do with the sins of the saints, the cleansing of the sanctuary, or Christ's ministry in the heavenly sanctuary. It is, they claim, a judgment against the little-horn power, nothing more.

A few slight problems arise with this argument. To begin, if the little horn and its activities were historical events that unfolded before the time of Christ (as those who identify the little horn with Antiochus Epiphanes insist), then this judgment, which is supposed to be solely against the little horn, started before Christ and continues past our day and into the future. Remember, according to the prophecy, this judgment leads to the establishment of God's kingdom (Daniel 7:26-28). So if this judgment is dealing with the little horn alone, and the little horn met its demise more than a century before Christ, and if this same judgment also leads to the Second Coming, which hasn't happened yet even in the twenty-first century, then the judgment begins in the second century B.C. and continues at least into the twenty-first century A.D. Although not logically impossible, the idea is hardly plausible.

One the other hand, for those who want to put the activity of the little horn off in the future, and who see the judgment being against some future power, there's still the problem of the gap between the fourth kingdom of pagan Rome, and this future little horn. *What happened to 2,000 or so years of history in between?* If the little horn depicts a future antichrist, then Daniel 7 needs to be interpreted like this: Babylon, Media-Persia, Greece, pagan Rome (followed by a 1,500-year gap that covers the time of the early church, the time of papal dominance, the Reformation, etc.), and finally a last-day antichrist power destroyed in a judgment that leads to the Second Coming. Again, although it's not impossible, such an interpretation just doesn't make sense, especially when nothing in Daniel 7 indicates such a massive gap in the prophecies.

Now, there is no question that as a *result* of the judgment, the little horn faces its demise. Nor can it be denied that the judgment is depicted *in the context* of the little horn and its activities. But neither of these facts neutralizes the pre-Advent judgment as Seventh-day Adventists understand it. On the contrary.

The first depiction of the judgment appears in Daniel 7:9, 10.

> I considered the horns, and, behold, there came up among them another little horn, before whom were three of the first horns plucked up by the roots: and, behold, in this horn were eyes like the eyes of a man, and a mouth speaking great things. I beheld till the thrones were cast down, and the Ancient of days did sit, whose garment was white as snow, and the hair of his head like the pure wool: his throne was like the fiery flame, and his wheels as burning fire. A fiery stream issued and came forth from before him: thousand thousands ministered unto him, and ten thousand times ten thousand stood before him: the judgment was set, and the books were opened (Daniel 7:8-10).

Notice that no direct cause-and-effect relationship is depicted here. Daniel describes the little-horn power and then shifts to the judgment in heaven. He tells about the little horn and then says, "I beheld . . ." and goes on to describe the thrones, the flames, the books, the judgment. The phrase, "I beheld" is his way of saying what he saw, of how it appeared to him *in his dream*. That is, he saw images of the Ancient of Days sitting; he saw His white garment, woolly hair, fiery thrones, and burning wheels. Again—and this is important—nothing here says that the judgment brings about the demise of the little horn, though in fact it does, which is no big deal because the judgment brings about the end of the whole world, at least as we know it, and that would include, of course, the end of the little-horn power as well. Nothing says, either, that the judgment is brought on by the activity of the little horn. No reason for the judgment is given.

The sequence comes again, this time in verses 20-22:

> And of the ten horns that were in his head, and of the other which came up, and before whom three fell; even of that horn that had eyes, and a mouth that spake very great things, whose look was more stout than his fellows. *I beheld,* and the same horn made war with the saints, and prevailed against them; Until the Ancient of days came, and judgment was given to the saints of the most High; and the time came that the saints possessed the kingdom (Daniel 7:20-22).

Here, again, the same events are shown, with a clear link between the activity of the little horn and the judgment in heaven. There's no question, then, from these verses, that whatever else the judgment includes, it does include something against the little-horn power. No one is denying that or even that the judgment ultimately leads to the demise of the little horn. As stated above, the judgment leads to the Second Coming, which ends every earthly power (Daniel 2:35, 44), including the little horn. The crucial point is that the judgment involves more than just judgment against the little horn.

In the first mention of the judgment in heaven (verses 8-14) Daniel described what he saw in the dream. "I beheld" he says (verse 9), describing what was shown him. In verses 15 and 16 Daniel then talks about how he felt after seeing the dream and introduces the heavenly being "who made me know the interpretation of the things" (verse16). In verse 17, the heavenly interpreter starts telling Daniel what the dream is about. In verses 17-20, Daniel is recounting what the interpreter told him—that there would be four kingdoms and that out of the fourth would arise a terrible little-horn power, which would "speak great things," etc.

Next, starting in verse 21, comes a shift from what Daniel was being told by the interpreter to *what Daniel saw in the dream*. He has now moved from angelic interpretation to his own description. "*I beheld,* and the same horn made war with the saints, and prevailed against them; Until the Ancient of days came, and judgment was given to the saints of the most High; and the time came that the saints possessed the kingdom" (verses 21, 22). Instead of writing about what he was told, Daniel writes about *what he saw,* about what *appeared to him.* "I beheld" the little horn do these things, he assures us, until the judgment took place.

Finally, in verse 23, the chapter shifts back again to the interpretation, with the angel explaining to Daniel the meaning of what he had seen in his dream: "Thus he [the angel interpreter] said, The fourth beast shall be the fourth kingdom. . . ."

So in Daniel 7:17-20, 23-27, it's all the angel interpreting for Daniel the meaning of the vision; however, verses 21 and 22, which talk about the relationship between the little-horn power and the judgment, are not interpretation, but merely Daniel's description of how the dream appeared to him.

This distinction is important. The whole chapter of Daniel 7 has only twenty-eight verses, and in those verses it covers the dream, the interpretation of the dream, as well as some of Daniel's distress at what he was shown. In other words, Daniel 7 covers the history of the world from Babylon until the Second Coming. More than 2,600 years of world history are swept over in just a few dozen verses, of which a good part are merely an interpretation of other verses. In such a situation, things, understandably, get crammed; not a lot of wiggle room is given to the author. If the time, times, and dividing of time ended in the late eighteenth and early nineteenth century, followed by a judgment that began, say within even fifty years or so, then it's not difficult to see why, *in the dream itself, in how it appeared to him,* Daniel would talk about the activity of the little horn going on *until* the judgment. From the end of the eighteenth or early nineteenth century to, say 1844, isn't a whole lot of time, not in a prophecy that covers more than 2,600 years in a few dozen verses that often repeat the same aspects of the prophecy. The use of "until" simply is showing how it appeared to Daniel; it was not an interpretation itself.

This point is clarified in *the interpretation* of what Daniel saw, which comes next:

> Thus he [the interpreter] said, The fourth beast shall be the fourth kingdom upon earth, which shall be diverse from all kingdoms, and shall devour the whole earth, and shall tread it down, and break it in pieces. And the ten horns out of this kingdom are ten kings that shall arise: and another shall rise after them; and he shall be diverse from the first, and he shall subdue three kings. And he shall speak great words against the most High, and shall wear out the saints of the most High, and think to change times and laws: and they shall be given into his hand until a time and times and the dividing of time. *But* the judgment shall sit, and they shall take away his dominion, to consume and to destroy it unto the end. And the kingdom and dominion, and the greatness of the kingdom under the whole heaven, shall be given to the people of the saints of the most High, whose kingdom is an everlasting kingdom, and all dominions shall serve and obey him (Daniel 7:23-27).

In the interpretation itself (as opposed to how it appeared to Daniel) the judgment is not depicted as some immediate response to the little-horn activity. That is, the judgment is not the event that ends the 1,260 years of persecution. The interpretation does not say that. The little horn's persecution, at least in that phrase, is depicted as "the time, times and dividing of time." That time comes and goes, and *then* the judgment will sit. The end of the 1,260 years, at least according to the interpretation given, is not caused by the judgment.

In fact, the word translated "but" in verse 26 ("*But* the judgment shall sit") is a single Hebrew letter that can be translated as "and" or "then," and it is used all through Daniel 7 to show a chronological progression of events as in Daniel 7:26. "*Then* the judgment will sit." "*And* the judgment will sit." There is the persecution, which lasts for a specific length of time, and then, afterward, the judgment. To say, dogmatically, that the judgment in heaven is what ends the 1,260-year period of persecution is to read more into the text than is there.

This point, however seemingly trivial, is important because some seek to limit the judgment to the little horn alone and to the ending of the specific time of persecution depicted by the "times, time and dividing of time." But that's not how the prophecy is explained by Daniel's interpreter. Though the little horn and the judgment are linked, one cannot say, at least from the interpretation itself, that the 1,260-year period was ended by the heavenly judgment.

## WHO'S JUDGED?

However, if the judgment is really about the saints, the heavenly sanctuary, and those who have professed faith in Christ, as Adventists teach, why is this judgment depicted in the context of the little horn?

Good question, and the answer, very briefly, can be found in the Hebrew concept of justice and judgment, which involves not only the vindication of the innocent but the punishment of the guilty, elements that appear in both Daniel 7 and 8. The little horn does its evil against God's people; ultimately, there is a judgment that not only vindicates the Lord's people—"and judgment was given *in favor of the saints*" (Daniel 7:22, italics supplied)—but that also brings the wicked to final justice—"the judgment shall sit, and they [the saints] shall take away his dominion, to consume and destroy it unto the end" (verse 26). In other words, in the context of the pre-Advent judgment (which is the work of Christ in our behalf in the heavenly judgment), the depiction of the demise of the little horn, the symbol of evil, makes perfect sense. It's no mystery that the vindication of the saints and the condemnation of the little horn are linked. It's typical in the Hebrew understanding of justice, judgment, and vindication; all occur together.

"If there be a controversy between men, and they come unto judgment, that the judges may judge them; then they shall justify the righteous, and condemn the wicked" (Deuteronomy 25:1). Here we see a fundamental principle of the biblical concept of justice, of judgment. It involves not *just* the punishment of the guilty or the vindication of the righteous. It contains both elements, as in Daniel. Judgment is given "to the saints," or even better, "in favor of the saints" in the judgment depicted in chapter 7 and elaborated on in chapter 8 (for the cleansing of the sanctuary involves judgment). And this judgment leads to the final demise of the antichrist power depicted in both chapters.

"Then hear thou in heaven, and do, and judge thy servants, condemning the wicked, to bring his way upon his head; and justifying the righteous, to give him according to his righteousness" (1 Kings 8:32). Here, in one verse, is the essence of what's depicted in both Daniel 7 and 8—the wicked punished, the righteous justified. This is judgment, and this is why both Daniel 7 and Daniel 8 depict the demise of the little-horn power, because in this judgment, not only are God's people vindicated, but the persecutor is punished.

Again, no one is denying that the *result* of the judgment brings about the final demise of the little horn (after all, it brings about the end of all earthly kingdoms); the judgment, which leads to the Second Coming, is simply not limited only to the end of the little horn, that's all. It's a much grander, broader event that leads to the vindication of the saints, as well as the demise of their (and God's) enemies. Writes Roy Gane of Andrews University:

> If there is a court case that results in one party winning and the other losing, it is because the two parties are opposed to each other. Through investigation, one is found to be right and the other wrong. The "horn" is opposed to Christ. It speaks arrogant words against "the Most High," oppresses His people, and intends to change God's law. The horn power is a rebel who claims control instead of Christ.
>
> When Christ wins in the judgment, His loyal people win with Him. They are delivered from the oppression of the horn and gain the kingdom: " . . .the Ancient One came; then judgment was given for the holy ones of the Most High and the time arrived when the holy ones gained possession of the kingdom" (Daniel 7:22; see also verse 27).
>
> Just as the Israelite high priest on the Day of Atonement repre-

sented his people before God, so Christ represents His people. Like the ancient Day of Atonement, the end-time judgment distinguishes between two groups. Those who are loyal to God and those who are not.[3]

This same principle is seen in Daniel 8. No question, there is a focus on the activity of the little-horn power; and there's no question, too, that the cleansing of the sanctuary brings about its demise. But that's only because on the antitypical day of atonement, judgment is given "to" or "in favor of" God's people (see Daniel 7:22). After all, they get the eternal kingdom.

This point can be seen especially in the question that is asked in verse 13: "Then I heard one saint speaking, and another saint said unto that certain saint which spake, How long shall be the vision *concerning* the daily sacrifice, and the transgression of desolation, to give both the sanctuary and the host to be trodden under foot?"

What's crucial is that the word "concerning" does not appear in the Hebrew, nor does Hebrew grammar allow for it. Thus the question isn't just about the activity of the little horn. Instead, the question is about everything depicted in the chapter, which includes the vision about the ram and the goat (Media-Persia and Greece) as well as the activity of the little horn (pagan and papal Rome). A literal translation would read, "How long the vision, the daily, and the transgression of desolation to give the sanctuary and the host a trampling." In other words, the question lists the things that happened in the vision. In fact, the word for "vision" in verse 13 is *hazon*, which deals with the ram and the goat, that is, Media-Persia and Greece (see the next chapter).

The question, then, could be paraphrased like this, *How long will all these things, from the rise of Media-Persia, the rise of Greece, and finally to Rome's attack on Christ's heavenly ministry, be allowed to go on?*

The answer, then, is that the sanctuary in heaven will be cleansed (or that the judgment in heaven will sit) at the end of the 2,300 years. And, of course, as a result of that judgment, the saints receive the kingdom (Daniel 7:26-28), and the little-horn power is judged and destroyed. The crucial point to see is that prophecy covers all the events of the chapter, which deal with the history of God's people from Media-Persia until the end of the age.

To repeat, in the Hebrew Bible judgment involved two things—the punishment of the wicked and the vindication of the righteous, the saints. Though that aspect is not explicitly stated in Daniel 8, as in Daniel 7, it comes through via (1) what the type teaches regarding the Day of Atonement and (2) the parallel between Daniel 7 and Daniel 8 (see below) where vindication of the saints is clearly shown in Daniel 7.

In short, those who get hung up on the demise of the little horn in Daniel 7 and 8, asserting that the judgment is only in reference to it, don't understand the Hebrew concept of judgment, which includes vindication of the righteous, along with the punishment of the wicked. What better depiction of the pre-Advent judgment, which results not only in the vindication of the saints, once and for all, but leads to the one event—the Second Coming—that brings about the final demise of the little-horn power?

These facts, then, virtually refute the so-called "context problem" of Daniel 7 and 8 (another retreaded Des Ford argument in Brother Dale's book[4]), which argues that the issue, especially in Daniel 8, deals only with the little horn, which didn't arise on the scene until long after the beginning of the 2,300 years, and thus Daniel 7 and 8 have nothing to do with some sort of heavenly pre-Advent judgment. The framing of the question in verse 13 shows that it's dealing with events that, though certainly including the little horn and its work of usurpation and persecution, also precede it, covering the whole scope of human history, starting with Media-Persia and culminating in the end of the world.

## DANIEL 8, AGAIN

Thus, we have seen in Daniel 7 that there's a massive judgment scene in heaven sometime after the 1,260 years of papal dominion, a judgment that leads to the second coming of Christ.

Now, we return to Daniel 8, which we looked at in the previous chapter. Let's first recap that chapter, because it's crucial to everything we believe.

Daniel has a vision of a ram, a goat, a little horn, and then is told that the sanctuary will be cleansed (Daniel 8:1-14).

Ram
Goat
Little horn
Sanctuary cleansed

Here's the essence of Daniel 8. Study that sequence until it's branded in your brain. Make it second nature; you won't be sorry.

As we saw too, in the interpretation (Daniel 8:20, 21), the ram is Media-Persia, the goat is Greece, and the little horn, though not named as were the ram and the goat, is solely, totally, and only Rome, both pagan and papal (although the emphasis is on the papal phase). The little horn can be nothing else; and, as we saw, Jesus and the New Testament help show us why.

Thus Daniel 8 could be summarized:

Media-Persia<br>
Greece<br>
Rome (pagan/papal)<br>
Sanctuary cleansed

Again the parallels between Daniel 2 and Daniel 7 and 8 are undeniable, even foundational. Let's look at them, this time including the element of the judgment, which appears so prominently in Daniel 7, and the cleansing of the sanctuary, which climaxes the vision of Daniel 8.

| Daniel 2 | Daniel 7 | Daniel 8 |
|---|---|---|
| Babylon | Babylon | —— |
| Media-Persia | Media-Persia | Media-Persia |
| Greece | Greece | Greece |
| Rome (pagan/papal) | Rome (pagan/papal) | Rome (pagan/papal) |
| —— | Judgment in heaven | Cleansing of the sanctuary |
| Second Coming | Second Coming | —— |

Look at the parallels:

Babylon in Daniel 2 and Babylon in Daniel 7.

Media-Persia in Daniel 2, Media-Persia in Daniel 7, Media-Persia in Daniel 8.

Greece in Daniel 2, Greece in Daniel 7, Greece in Daniel 8.

Rome in Daniel 2, Rome in Daniel 7, Rome in Daniel 8.

Then, in Daniel 7, after Rome, the judgment scene in heaven appears, and it directly parallels the cleansing of the sanctuary, which in Daniel 8 arises after Rome as well. In short, this massive heavenly judgment scene in Daniel 7, the judgment that leads to the end of the world, is the same thing as the cleansing of the sanctuary in Daniel 8. We are given here two different depictions of the same thing: the pre-Advent judgment (for it's clear that the judgment in Daniel 7 occurs before the Second Coming), also known as the cleansing of the sanctuary, in Daniel 8.

Finally, both Daniel 2 and Daniel 7 specifically talk about the end of the world, at least this present world, and that happens at the Second Coming.

The crucial point is the parallel between this massive judgment scene in Daniel 7 and the cleansing of the sanctuary in Daniel 8. I can't stress how important this parallel is. The judgment scene in Daniel 7 is simply another way of expressing the cleansing of the sanctuary in Daniel 8, just as the depiction of the bear in Daniel 7 is another way of expressing the ram in Daniel 8. Each depiction adds to the other, elaborating on each other, together giving us a lot of information about the specific event.

Study these parallels until they become a fundamental part of your Adventist faith. Using your Bible alone, make your own chart, until you can see not only the sequence of events, but the parallel between the judgment scene in Daniel 7 and the cleansing of the sanctuary in Daniel 8. Grounded in this, you'll be on a foundation as solid as world history itself.

And there's more. As I touched on in *1844 Made Simple*, the Jewish understanding of the Day of Atonement (known as Yom Kippur), the day when the sanctuary is cleansed, is that of judgment. Here's a quote from a Jewish source on what happens during the Day of Atonement, the cleansing of the sanctuary: "God is seated on His throne to judge the world. Simultaneously the judge, pleader, expert, and witness, openeth the Book of Records, and it is read, every man's signature being found therein. The great trumpet is sounded; a still small voice is heard; the angels shudder, saying, this is the day of judgment."[5] Sounds like the judgment scene in Daniel 7!

Dr. Jacques Doukhan, a Jew and professor at Andrews University Seminary, writing about Daniel 7 and 8 and the cleansing of the sanctuary in Daniel 8:14, states:

> According to the parallelism between the two chapters, the events described in Daniel 8 as the cleansing (or the reconsecration) of the sanctuary would then correspond to the day of judgment in chap-

ter 7. Significantly, the Septuagint [a Greek translation of the Hebrew Bible made before the time of Christ] translates this term with
the Greek word *katharisai* (to purify), a technical word used to refer
to Kippur. The great Jewish commentator Rashi also suggested that
we should read this passage [Daniel 8:14] in the context of the Day
of Atonement.

What chapter 7 calls the Day of Judgment chapter 8 labels as the
Day of Atonement. They are in fact the same event. Israel experienced the Day of Atonement as the actualization of the last judgment.[6]

After I became an Adventist and read *The Great Controversy*, I was
amazed at Ellen White's description of the pre-Advent judgment because
it sounded just like what the Jews believe happens on the Day of Atonement, Yom Kippur. That's not surprising because, clearly, Daniel 8 shows
that the pre-Advent judgment scene in heaven is another depiction of
the cleansing of the sanctuary, the Day of Atonement, in Daniel 8. They
are simply two different depictions of the same thing, one focusing directly on the judgment aspect, the other introducing the element of the
heavenly sanctuary (what other sanctuary could it be, given the context, which is the judgment at the end of the world?). They are shown
parallel to each other because the Lord wants us to study them with the
light each one shines on the other, and together they present what we
understand as the pre-Advent judgment, an event that has, literally,
worldwide implications.

Indeed, Daniel 8 consists of four elements: Media-Persia, Greece, pa-
gan/papal Rome, and the cleansing of the sanctuary. Just four.

Now, the first element, Media-Persia, certainly played an important
role in the history of the world and the history of God's people. Media-
Persia freed the Jews from Babylonian captivity and paved the way for the
re-establishment of the Hebrew nation. Greece, too, affected the world
and the church in a big way. In fact, Greek thought remains a powerful
influence in the world even today. The third element, Rome, of course
played a major role in the world and with God's people, a role that will
continue up until the Second Coming.

Now (and here's the crucial point), if only four elements exist in the
chapter, and the first three are significant enough to have literally worldwide impact, what does that automatically say about the fourth element,
the cleansing of the sanctuary?

Of course, it must be of major significance too!

Why would the Lord link these three behemoths with something that itself wasn't of gargantuan significance? He didn't. The cleansing of the sanctuary—which all but climaxes the vision of Daniel 8—is, obviously, something of major importance, on a par with, or even superseding, the great powers that precede it in the vision! And what could that be?

Of course—it's the great judgment that leads to the Second Coming and the establishment of God's eternal kingdom, all so clearly shown in Daniel 7. That's why the cleansing of the sanctuary is listed with the three major kingdoms preceding it, because the 2,300 days talk about the event that will, ultimately, lead to the last, and final kingdom—God's kingdom, the one greater than all those that preceded it.

Thus, even if someone wanted to argue against the Adventist interpretation of Daniel 8:14, the context alone demands that whatever interpretation one chooses, it must be seen as an event having major implications for the world and God's people, as did all the other elements in the prophecy. And as far as I know, Adventists are the only people in the world who give any significance at all to Daniel 8:14. For most of the Christian world, it's seen as nothing but a description of Antiochus Epiphanes.

And, finally, as we saw earlier, Babylon ended about the early-to-mid sixth century B.C. After Babylon was Media-Persia, whose hegemony lasted from the early-to-mid sixth century to the early-to-mid fourth century B.C. After Media-Persia came Greece, which flourished from about the early-to-mid fourth century to the mid-second century B.C. And then there's Rome. First, the pagan phase, which rose to the height of its power about mid-second century B.C. until collapsing about the fifth to the sixth century A.D. Next is papal Rome, which according to the first prophetic *time* prophecy in Daniel, has hegemony for 1,260 years, following the collapse of pagan Rome, which means that the papal phase of Rome, as depicted in Daniel 7, extended from the sixth century A.D. to the eighteenth to nineteenth century A.D. Then, it was *after* this prophetic time prophecy, after this specific phase of papal Rome, that the judgment scene in heaven takes place.

Thus, what's clear so far from Daniel 7 is that the judgment scene in heaven, a judgment that leads to the establishment of God's kingdom, occurs sometime *after* the 1,260 years of papal persecution, sometime after the *late* eighteenth or early nineteenth century.

Now, if the cleansing of the sanctuary in Daniel 8 is the same thing as this judgment scene in heaven as shown in Daniel 8 (which it is), and if the judgment scene in heaven began sometime after the late eighteenth or early nineteenth century (which it did), then the cleansing of the sanctuary in Daniel 8 began sometime after the late eighteenth or early nineteenth century, too, because they are the same thing.

| Daniel 7 | Daniel 8 |
|---|---|
| Babylon | |
| (Ends early-to-mid sixth century B.C.) | |
| Media-Persia | Media-Persia |
| (From early-to-mid sixth century to early-to-mid fourth century B.C.) | |
| Greece | Greece |
| (From early-to-mid fourth century to mid-second century B.C.) | |
| Pagan Rome | Pagan Rome |
| (From mid-second century B.C. to fifth-to-sixth century A.D.) | |
| Papal Rome | Papal Rome |
| (From sixth century A.D. to eighteenth-nineteenth century A.D.) | |
| Judgment in heaven | Cleansing of the sanctuary |
| Second Coming | Destroyed without hands |

A massive judgment scene in heaven (Daniel 7), depicted in the context of the cleansing of the heavenly sanctuary (Daniel 7), which happens sometime after the late eighteenth and early nineteenth century, but before the Second Coming. Sound familiar? Of course. It sounds like the judgment that Brother Dale has worked so assiduously to deny.

Again, study these points until they become chiseled into your mind. The key is to see the sequence of kingdoms, and then the parallel between them, showing beyond doubt that the judgment scene in Daniel 7 is the same thing as the cleansing of the sanctuary in Daniel 8. Get grounded in that until you can see it without equivocation. Again, I can't stress how much this foundation will ground you in this aspect of our message.

With this background, we're ready to examine more of Brother Dale's arguments against the pre-Advent judgment, the judgment that's so clearly depicted in the texts above.

---

[1] *CDSDA,* pp. 167, 168.

[2] Thomas Hobbes, *Leviathan,* in *Great Books of the Western World* (Chicago: Encyclopedia Britannica, 1971), p. 278.

[3] Roy Gane, *Altar Call* (Diadem, Berrien Springs, MI) 1999, p. 241.

[4] *CDSDA,* p. 174, 175.

[5] "Atonement," *Jewish Encyclopedia,* vol. 2., p. 286.

[6] Jacques Doukhan, *Secrets of Daniel* (Review and Herald; Hagerstown, MD ) 2000, p. 127.

# CHAPTER FIVE

# WEAKEST

# LINKS?

Imagine someone in the twenty-first century justifying the legacy of Joseph Stalin and the communist system of the former Soviet Union. Imagine this person declaring that Soviet-style Marxism was the best way to free workers from oppression, to spread wealth among the masses, and to ensure liberty and equality among all people. Imagine this person declaring that, due to the natural flow of history, the state will wither away, capitalism will vanish because of its own internal contradictions, and the world will evolve into a pure communist utopia.

Now there was a time in the past when—without the benefit of what we now know—secular people could have been excused for seeking hope in the Marxist ideal. But, today, after the communist legacy has been exposed for the oppressive sham it always had been, such sentiments are inexcusable.

This is how I feel about Brother Dale's biblical arguments against the investigative judgment. Most are recycled challenges posed by Dr. Desmond Ford about two decades ago, challenges that, at the time, were worthy of serious responses. Today, however, these challenges have long been answered by leading Adventist scholars, and yet Brother Dale ignores those answers and instead repeats the same tired, old lines—lines that sound to those who have studied them like someone today claiming that social, political, historical, and economic truth is found in the communist worldview.

Nevertheless, because the challenges are there, and because answering them can only strengthen our belief in the investigative judgment, let's take a look at some of these objections. I'm not going to deal with all of them (some are not relevant; some have already been answered in previous chapters) nor am I going to address the challenges in the same order that Brother Ratzlaff does. Instead, I have two goals: first, to show how flimsy these biblical arguments are (as we did regarding our brother's claim that the little horn of Daniel 8 is Antiochus Ephiphanes); second, to present even more evidence that we Adventists are on firm, biblical ground regarding the 1844 investigative judgment.

## SEVENTY WEEKS

Taking his cues from Desmond Ford's massive (and now discredited) *Daniel 8:14, The Day of Atonement, and the Investigative Judgment,*[1] Brother Ratzlaff attacks the idea that "the 2300 years begin at the same time as the seventy weeks."[2] In other words, he's attacking the tenet, crucial to our belief, that the seventy-week prophecy of Daniel 9 is linked to the 2,300 days of Daniel 8:14. Dr. Ford has been trying for years to sever that link; Brother Dale (perhaps in ignorance of the answers) simply reiterates Dr. Ford's failed endeavors.

I dealt in a general manner with the link between the two chapters in *1844 Made Simple.* For a much deeper, and more scholarly, approach I recommend volume 2 of the Daniel and Revelation Committee Series *(Symposium on Daniel),* where, in a chapter titled "The 'Little Horn', the Heavenly Sanctuary, and the Time of the End: A Study of Daniel 8:9-14,"[3] the late Dr. Gerhard Hasel deals with links between Daniel 8 and 9 (see especially pages 436–444). Also, in the same volume, Dr. William Shea ("Unity of Daniel") not only *writes* that "the visions of chapters 8 and 9 are closely linked, being for all practical purposes one vision"[4]—he *proves* that they are. Brother Dale has listed both books in his bibliography, but ignores the arguments in them.

Thus, can we justify our assertion that the seventy weeks of Daniel 9:24-27 are linked to the 2,300 days of Daniel 8:14?

To begin, Daniel 2, Daniel 7, and Daniel 8 are chapters that consist of dreams and/or visions followed by an interpretation of that dream or vision, though in Daniel 8 the interpretation was incomplete. In contrast,

Daniel 9, unlike these other previous chapters, has no dreams or visions; it consists, after Daniel's prayer, only of an interpretation—the seventy-week prophecy given to him by Gabriel.

Here's how Daniel depicts the arrival of Gabriel:

> Yea, whiles I was speaking in prayer, even the man Gabriel, whom I had seen in the vision at the beginning, being caused to fly swiftly, touched me about the time of the evening oblation. And he informed me, and talked with me, and said, O Daniel, I am *now come forth to give thee skill and understanding.* At the beginning of thy supplications the commandment came forth, and *I am come to shew thee;* for thou art greatly beloved: *therefore understand the matter,* and consider the vision (Daniel 9:21-23, italics supplied).

Notice the three italicized sections in the above verses; all express Gabriel's intent to explain something to Daniel, to give him understanding, to show him something. As we'll see, he came to interpret for Daniel the one part of the vision in chapter 8—the 2,300 days—that was not already interpreted for him.

The vision in Daniel 8 consists of the ram, the goat, the little horn, and the sanctuary being cleansed (the 2,300 days). The ram was interpreted, the goat was interpreted, and the little horn was interpreted (Daniel 8:19-25); the only part of the vision that wasn't interpreted was the part dealing with the 2,300 days, the part Daniel said that he didn't understand.

Listen carefully to what Daniel says here:

> And the vision of the evening and the morning which was told is true: wherefore shut thou up the vision; for it shall be for many days. And I Daniel fainted, and was sick certain days; afterward I rose up, and did the king's business; and I was astonished at the vision, but none understood it (Daniel 8:26, 27).

A few salient facts will make our position obvious. First, when Gabriel talks about the vision of the "evening and morning" in the above text, he is talking about Daniel 8:14, which reads (more literally), "Until evening morning 2,300. . . ." Gabriel's reference, then, in verse 26, to the vision of the "evening and morning" (which he stresses is "true") points specifically to the 2,300 days of Daniel 8:14. Daniel said that he didn't understand it, that is, he didn't understand the vision about the 2,300 days, which isn't surprising because everything else in chapter 8 had been explained.

Also, two different Hebrew words are translated "vision" in Daniel 8. In verses 1 and 2, Daniel three times makes reference to the "vision" of the chapter, and each time it comes from the same Hebrew word, *hazon*: "In the third year of the reign of king Belshazzar *a vision (hazon)* appeared unto me, even unto me Daniel, after that which appeared unto me at the first. And I saw in *a vision (hazon)*; and it came to pass, when I saw, that I was at Shushan in the palace, which is in the province of Elam, and I saw in a *vision (hazon)*, and I was by the river of Ulai" (Daniel 8:1, 2).

Daniel then describes what he sees in the *hazon:* the ram, the goat, the little horn, etc. *Hazon,* therefore, refers to the general vision of chapter 8.

In contrast, when he talks specifically about the 2,300 days, Daniel uses a different word for vision, *mareh*. "And the vision [*mareh*] of the evening and the morning which was told is true . . . And I Daniel fainted, and was sick certain days; afterward I rose up, and did the king's business; and I was astonished at the vision [*mareh*], but none understood it" (Daniel 8:26, 27).[5]

Thus, we have two words for "vision" in Daniel 8: *hazon* for the whole vision, and *mareh* for Daniel 8:14, the vision about the 2,300 days and the sanctuary being cleansed—the part that Daniel didn't understand (Daniel 8:27).

Now, these two words appear again, in Daniel 9, when Gabriel appears to Daniel after his prayer.

> Yea, whiles I was speaking in prayer, even the man Gabriel, whom I had seen in the vision [*hazon*] at the beginning, being caused to fly swiftly, touched me about the time of the evening oblation. And he informed me, and talked with me, and said, O Daniel, I am now come forth to give thee skill and understanding. At the beginning of thy supplications the commandment came forth, and I am come to shew thee; for thou art greatly beloved: therefore understand the matter, and consider the vision [*mareh*] (Daniel 9:21-23).

Notice, Daniel refers to Gabriel, the angel he had seen in the *hazon* of Daniel 8 (Gabriel is the one who, in Daniel 8:16, is told to explain to Daniel the vision). Notice, too, that Gabriel comes to Daniel and says that he's here to give him "skill and understanding." Skill and understanding about what? The last time we left Daniel, he didn't understand the *mareh* of Daniel 8:14.

It's interesting, too, that the Hebrew word translated "understanding" in 9:22 is derived from the same Hebrew root word (*bin*) Daniel used in 8:27, when he said he was astonished at the *mareh* and "none understood [*bin*] it" (Daniel 8:27). Thus, it seems that Gabriel appears in chapter 9 to give Daniel the *bin*, the understanding, that he didn't have in chapter 8.

This point becomes even clearer when we examine the word for "vision" that Gabriel uses in verse 23 just before giving Daniel the seventy-week prophecy. Look at this carefully: "At the beginning of thy supplications the commandment came forth, and I am come to shew thee; for thou art greatly beloved: therefore understand the matter, and consider the vision [*mareh*]."

*Mareh*? What *mareh*? There's only one, the *mareh* of the 2,300 evenings and mornings in 8:14 that Daniel didn't understand. We have the same angel interpreter as in the *hazon* of Daniel 8, to which Daniel himself refers when Gabriel first appears. Gabriel then promises to give Daniel *bin* (understanding), and the last time we saw Daniel needing *bin* was in reference to the 2,300 evening and mornings of Daniel 8:14. Gabriel then points him specifically to the *mareh* and tells him to "consider" it ("consider" also comes from *bin*).

Another point. What kind of prophecy was the *mareh* of Daniel 8:14? It was a time prophecy. What is the first thing that Gabriel gives to Daniel? Of course, a time prophecy—the seventy weeks—that he begins to explain in Daniel 9:24.

Without question, Gabriel comes to Daniel in chapter 9 in order to give him the explanation about the 2,300 days in chapter 8.

Adventists aren't the only ones to see this link, either. I have in my office an orthodox Jewish commentary on Daniel. What's amazing is how this commentary handles the seventy weeks of Daniel 9:24-27. Below is the extract on the phrase "consider the *mareh*," though this commentary translates it "gain understanding of the vision," a more accurate rendition of the verb in the phrase (*bin* in the *hiphil*). What does this Jewish commentary do with the seventy-week prophecy?

This refers to Daniel's vision in chapter 8 in which the part that disturbed him so (v. 14) is characterized in vs. 16-26 as a mareh.[6]

The first thing it does is to point it back to Daniel 8:14. In other words, the Jews, who certainly don't have the same "agenda" as Adventists, nevertheless see the same link between Daniel 8:14 and the seventy-week prophecy of Daniel 9:24-27.

Does this commentary prove the link between the two chapters? Of course not. What it does prove, though, is that others, not just Adventists, see the tie between the two chapters—because it's there, despite the best efforts of Dr. Ford and Brother Dale to deny it.

## CUT OFF

Any attack on the link between Daniel 8:14 and Daniel 9:24-27 comes with the mandatory mantra against the Adventist understanding of Daniel 9:24, particularly the beginning phrase, "Seventy weeks are determined upon thy people. . . ." Brother Dale, again taking his cue directly from Des Ford, argues that "there is no way of proving that the cutting off of the 490 from 2300 is intended."[7]

Now, with your Bible open, let's look at what we have here in Daniel 9:24. To begin, we've seen the undeniable link between the two time prophecies, the *mareh* of the 2,300 days of Daniel 8:14 and the appearance of Gabriel in Daniel 9, which introduces the seventy-week prophecy. How interesting, too, that the *mareh* of Daniel 8:14, unlike the rest of the *hazon,* constitutes an audition, something that Daniel *hears,* as opposed to something he *sees,* as in the rest of the vision. Read Daniel 8; the *mareh* of the 2,300 days is revealed in words, not in visible symbols. In Daniel 9, when Gabriel returns and gives him the explanation, he doesn't give Daniel a vision of rams, goats, little horns, etc.; he gives him something to hear, an audition, as with the *mareh* of chapter 8.

Gabriel comes to Daniel, calls his attention back to the 2,300 days, and then immediately points him to another time prophecy, one that is, at least on the surface, shorter than the *mareh* of Daniel 8 (seventy weeks is certainly less than 2,300 days). Thus, there's an immediate juxtaposition between these two numbers.

Let's use an analogy. Suppose you're a man and you and your wife have $1,000 in your bank account. Your wife comes to you and makes a direct reference to the $1,000, then mentions a lamp that costs $250. What's the immediate implication? She wants to pull $250 from the $1,000 for the lamp, right? Of course!

Let's use another analogy (a little less sexist). You tell your neighbor that you have five free hours on Sunday. The neighbor comes over and, after making a direct reference to your five free hours, mentions that he needs someone to help paint a room. "It will take only an hour," he says. What's the immediate implication of his juxtaposing the one hour against the five? Of course—one of those hours should be taken out to help him paint.

Now, again, Daniel 8 and 9. After making a direct reference to the 2,300 evenings and mornings, the angel immediately gives Daniel a shorter time prophecy, the seventy weeks, juxtaposing one against the other. What's the immediate implication? Of course—that the seventy-week prophecy is part of, or should be taken from, the larger one of 2,300 days.

Brother Dale admits that the verb in Daniel 9:24, "Seventy weeks *are decreed*" can also mean cut, as in "cut off." He writes, "*Chatchak* means 'cut' or 'decree. . . .' "[8]

That the seventy weeks are cut off from, or taken out of, the 2,300 days is made even more apparent by the verb *chatchak* itself. This is a *hapax legomenon,* a technical term for a word that appears only once in the Bible. This means we have no other instances to compare it with. Nevertheless, most Hebrew lexicons give one of the meanings, often the primary meaning, as "cut off." I own three Hebrew lexicons: *Gesenius* translates *chatchak* as "properly TO CUT, TO DIVIDE," with the idea of issuing a decree. *Brown, Driver and Briggs* defines it as "divide, determine." Holladay (an abridged lexicon) defines it as "decreed, ordained." Though not used anywhere else in the Bible, the verb appears in later Hebrew, and in a majority of cases it means "to cut off."

Years ago, in graduate school, I was studying Ugaritic, a language similar to Hebrew (it used cuneiform wedges as opposed to Hebrew Script). I remember studying a Ugaritic poem and coming across *chatchak* in the text, which was translated "cut off." Excited I called one of our Ancient Near Eastern scholars and said, jokingly, "I've found the text that will save Adventism!" However, I was too late. Other scholars had already noted the link between *chatchak* in both languages, giving more evidence that "cut off" is a valid meaning, if not *the* primary meaning, of the verb.

Look at the context, look at the analogies. We're given two time prophecies, the big one comes first, then the smaller one, which is introduced (in the context of the bigger) by a verb that has the basic meaning "to cut off." Is it, then, an outrageous conclusion to assume that the smaller number, the seventy weeks, is cut off from the larger one, the 2,300 days? Hardly. It is, in fact, the only logical conclusion.

And though "cut off" is the basic meaning of chatchak, "decreed" shouldn't be ignored either. Perhaps chatchak was used—as opposed to a word that meant exclusively "to cut off," or to a word that meant exclusively "decreed" (both are available in Hebrew)—in order to bring out both ideas, that of cutting off and decreeing. The seventy weeks, cut off from the 2,300 days, are decreed upon the Jewish nation to fulfill certain requirements.

What, then, of Brother Dale's (and Dr. Ford's) claim that there is "no way of proving that the cutting off of the 490 from the 2300 is intended"? The response, I guess, is what do you mean by "prove?" I doubt that Brother Dale or Brother Des can "prove" Jesus is the Messiah the way that they can "prove" 2 + 2 = 4. We're dealing with faith issues here. In such cases, there is little "proof" about anything—if by proof we mean scientific proof (though it's questionable whether even science absolutely "proves" anything). I don't know what Brother Dale or Dr. Ford mean by "prove," but one thing is certain: We can "prove" that our arguments for the seventy weeks being cut off from the 2,300 days are much better, stronger, and more firmly grounded than are theirs against it.

## 1,150 OR 2,300?

Dealing with this next argument makes me feel as if I'm dealing with the claim that Jesus changed the Sabbath to Sunday. It's one of those been-there-done-that kind of things. Nevertheless, no matter how often we have been there and done that (I dealt with this in *1844 Made Simple*), it's important to answer these charges, if for no other reason than to show the weak arguments that appear in the only chapter of Brother Ratzlaff's book that deals specifically with the biblical evidence against the pre-Advent judgment, arguments whose weaknesses epitomize Brother Dale's entire book.

Brother Dale asserts that the 2,300 evenings and mornings of Daniel 8:14 are really just 1,150 days. Why? Because the phrase "evening and morning" refers (he claims) to the daily sacrifice, and because there were two sacrifices per day, 2,300 sacrifices means only 1,150 days.

Is there any validity to this charge?

For years I have been using an incredible CD-rom Bible concordance, *Bible Works for Windows*. I couldn't live without it. On the next page are all the English translations of Daniel 8:14 on that version of *Bible Works for Windows*:

And he said unto me, Unto two thousand and three hundred days; then shall the sanctuary be cleansed (King James Version).

And he said unto me, Unto two thousand and three hundred evenings and mornings; then shall the sanctuary be cleansed (American Standard Version).

And he said to me, "For 2,300 evenings and mornings; then the holy place will be properly restored" (New American Standard).

He said to me, "For 2,300 evenings and mornings; then the holy place will be properly restored" (New American Bible).

And he said to him, "For two thousand and three hundred evenings and mornings; then the sanctuary shall be restored to its rightful state" (Revised Standard Version).

And he answered him, "For two thousand three hundred evenings and mornings; then the sanctuary shall be restored to its rightful state" (New Revised Standard).

And he said to me, "For two thousand three hundred days; then the sanctuary shall be cleansed" (New King James).

And he said to me, Until two thousand and three hundred days; then shall the sanctuary be cleansed (World English Bible).

And he said to me, Until two thousand and three hundred days; then shall the sanctuary be cleansed (Revised Webster's Bible).

And he said unto me, Until two thousand and three hundred evenings {and} mornings: then shall the sanctuary be vindicated (Douay).

And he said to him, For two thousand, three hundred evenings and mornings; then the holy place will be made clean (Bible in Basic English).

And he saith unto me, Till evening—morning two thousand and three hundred, then is the holy place declared right (Young's Literal Translation).

Notice that none translated the text as 1,150 days. My two versions of the Septuagint (an ancient Greek translation of the Hebrew Bible that dates to pre-Christian times) both translate Daniel 8:14 as "2300." The Vulgate, an early Latin edition of the Hebrew Bible, translates it "2300."

I've found only one version, the TEV, which uses the 1,150 days. Yet 1,150 isn't a translation; it's an interpretation, one based on the premise that Daniel 8 is dealing with Antiochus Ephiphanes. The problem, however, is that 2,300 days, even if taken literally, is six years, four months, and twenty days, while Antiochus's profanation of the temple, supposedly the focus of Daniel 8 and the little horn, lasted three years to the day, or (using a 360-day calendar) 1,080 days. Thus, the 2,300 days doesn't fit—not even close. So, instead, supporters of the idea divide the 2,300 days in half, which comes to 1,150 days—closer but still seventy days off.

Brother Dale, in asserting that the evidence for Antiochus as the little horn is "overwhelming," also writes that some scholars believe the book of Daniel "must have been written after 165 B.C., because it describes the persecutions of Antiochus with such exact detail."[9] If Daniel was, indeed, written after the fact, why didn't the author do a better job in getting the time element right? On the other hand, if the book is inspired by God, certainly He could have done a better job with the numbers, couldn't He? The problem, of course, isn't with the numbers; it's with the interpretation of the little horn as Antiochus.

Even putting Antiochus aside, the 1,150-day argument is based on the notion that the text refers to the *tamid,* or daily sanctuary sacrifice, offered twice a day. However, and Dr. Hasel expounds on this in detail, this sacrifice is always depicted in the sequence of *morning* before *evening,* never (as in Daniel 8:14) "evening morning." In other words, the sequence in Daniel 8 is opposite to the sequence used in every reference to the daily service. "No exception," wrote Hasel, "to the sequence appears in the OT."[10] Thus, if Daniel 8:14 was talking about the daily sacrifice, why didn't it use the same sequence as every Old Testament reference to the daily sacrifice? The answer, of course, is that it's not talking about the sacrifice, thus, there's no justification for halving the 2,300 days. In addition, the daily sanctuary sacrifice is viewed in Scripture as only one sacrifice that happens twice a day, showing that the division into two sacrifices is unwarranted.

Though the sequence, evening-morning in Daniel 8:14, is the opposite of the way the daily sacrifice is referred to, it *is* the same sequence found in the Genesis 1 Creation account regarding each day of Creation.

"And the *evening* and *morning* were the first *day*. . . ." "And the *evening* and *morning* were the second *day*" . . . "And the *evening* and *morning* were the third *day* . . ." Notice, the sequence, evening-morning, as in Daniel 8:14, and notice, too, how that sequence is related to the word "day."

Thus, contrary to Bother Dale and Dr. Ford, there's no basis to believe that the 2,300 "evening mornings" of Daniel 8:14 is anything other than how most every Bible has translated it, that is, as 2,300 days.

## CLEANSED

Another argument Brother Dale uses—no matter how consistently and frequently debunked—declares that it is incorrect to translate Daniel 8:14 as "cleansed" ("Unto 2300 days, then shall the sanctuary be cleansed"). This is another argument based on Dr. Ford and is an attempt to deny the link between Daniel 8:14 and the Levitical Day of Atonement when the earthly sanctuary was cleansed, thus denuding (if not altogether destroying) the Adventist claim that Daniel 8:14 is about the cleansing of the heavenly sanctuary.

Good work has been done in response to this question, work that Brother Dale has ignored.

As a start, go back to the previous section and look at the various translations of Daniel 8:14. Some, not all, translate it as "cleansed," evidence that at least some people have seen "cleansed" as an accurate translation of the verse. Many other older versions use "cleansed," and more recently the NAB has translated it "shall be purified." Indeed the new Jewish Publication Society Bible translates it as "cleansed."

Although the verb (*tsadaq*), translated "cleansed" in Daniel 8:14, appears more than five hundred times in the Old Testament, it appears only once is this specific verb form, the *niphil* or passive. It's used in various ways:

First, it appears as a legal term dealing with the vindication of the innocent and the punishment of the wicked. Look at these texts: "The Lord shall judge the people: judge me, O Lord, according to my *righteousness* [from *tsadaq*] and according to mine integrity that is in me. Oh let the wickedness of the wicked come to an end; but establish the *just* [from *tsadaq*]: for the *righteous* [from *tsadaq*] God trieth the hearts and reins" (Psalm 7:8, 9).

*Tsadaq* appears also in the context of salvation: "The Lord hath made known his salvation: his *righteousness* [from *tsadaq*] hath he openly shewed in the sight of the heathen" (Psalm 98:2). "He shall see of the travail of his soul, and shall be satisfied: by his knowledge shall my righteous servant *justify* [from *tsadaq*] many; for he shall bear their iniquities" (Isaiah 53:11).

It carries, as well, the idea of purification, of cleansing: "Shall mortal man be more *just* [from *tsadaq*] than God? shall a man be more *pure* [from the same word used in Leviticus for the cleansing of the sanctuary] than his maker?" (Job 4:17).

"We notice," writes Adventist Old Testament scholar Angel Rodriguez, "that the term *tsadaq* is associated with such concepts as judgment, vindication, cleansing, and salvation. The term conveys the idea of restoration of the order established by God through a work of cleansing and judgment"[11]—concepts directly related to what happens on the Day of Atonement, a day of judgment, vindication, salvation and, of course, cleansing.

No wonder the Septuagint, along with the Latin Vulgate, translates *tsadaq* as "cleansed" in Daniel 8:14. In fact, the Septuagint uses the same Greek word in Daniel 8:14 as it uses in Leviticus 16 when the chapter talks about the cleansing of the earthly sanctuary on the Day of Atonement. This especially makes sense when one examines the language of Daniel 8, which is saturated with concepts and images from the Old Testament sanctuary service, including the Day of Atonement.

Why Daniel didn't use the same specific Hebrew word for "cleansed" that appears in Leviticus is open for speculation. Had he done so, the argument against the link between Daniel 8:14 and the Levitical Day of Atonement would be moot. Enough other evidence exists, however, to show the link to Leviticus and the Day of Atonement which is why "cleansed" is an accurate translation. Perhaps when one considers the issue involved here—the final judgment that ends this world and ushers in the next (as revealed by the parallel between Daniel 7 and 8)—*tsadaq* was used because the verse deals with issues that are bigger than those conveyed by just the particular sanctuary word for "cleansing." The Lord employed a term that encapsulates more than a religious ritual. He sought to expand our minds to the largeness of what's happening here. And what's happening here, as we have seen, is that Daniel 8:14 parallels the judgment scene in Daniel 7—and in Jewish thinking the judgment occurred on the Day of Atonement, the day that the sanctuary was "cleansed."

Thus, to cavalierly dismiss the idea of "cleansing" or the Levitical link to Daniel 8:14 (as Brother Dale does) is, simply, wrong. We—along with those who translated the Septuagint, the Vulgate, the King James, and many other Bible versions as well—are on solid ground to maintain that "cleansed" is an accurate translation in Daniel 8:14.

## HEAVENLY OR EARTHLY?

Brother Dale, again based directly on Dr. Ford, argues against the Adventist position that "the sanctuary of Daniel 8:14 means the sanctuary in heaven," maintaining instead that "the context is about the sanctuary on earth."[12]

Here, too, the Antiochus interpretation is just assumed. If Daniel 8 were about this minor pagan ruler's attack against the Jews, Jerusalem, and the temple, then the context would indeed be the sanctuary on the earth. But, as we've seen, Antiochus can't be made to fit.

Instead, return to the parallels between Daniel 7 and 8. Study the chart; I can't stress how crucial this parallel is:

| Daniel 2 | Daniel 7 | Daniel 8 |
|---|---|---|
| Babylon | Babylon | —— |
| Media-Persia | Media-Persia | Media-Persia |
| Greece | Greece | Greece |
| Pagan (pagan/papal) | Pagan (pagan/papal) | Pagan (pagan/papal) |
| —— | Judgment in heaven | Cleansing of the sanctuary |
| Second Coming | Second Coming | —— |

The cleansing of the sanctuary in Daniel 8:14 is the same thing as the judgment scene in Daniel 7, the judgment that leads to the Second Coming at the end of this world. Look at that judgment itself, as it's depicted in prophecy:

> I beheld till the thrones were cast down, and the Ancient of days did sit, whose garment was white as snow, and the hair of his head like the pure wool: his throne was like the fiery flame, and his wheels as burning fire. A fiery stream issued and came forth from before him: thousand thousands ministered unto him, and ten thousand times ten thousand stood before him: the judgment was set, and the books were opened . . . . I saw in the night visions, and, behold, one like the Son of man came with the clouds of heaven, and came

to the Ancient of days, and they brought him near before him. And there was given him dominion, and glory, and a kingdom, that all people, nations, and languages, should serve him: his dominion is an everlasting dominion, which shall not pass away, and his kingdom that which shall not be destroyed. . . . But the judgment shall sit, and they shall take away his dominion, to consume and to destroy it unto the end. And the kingdom and dominion, and the greatness of the kingdom under the whole heaven, shall be given to the people of the saints of the most High, whose kingdom is an everlasting kingdom, and all dominions shall serve and obey him (Daniel 7:9,10, 13, 14, 26, 27).

Thrones, the Ancient of Days, the Son of man, fiery streams, books open, judgment—if this isn't a picture of something in heaven, what is? Something is happening in heaven that directly affects what happens on earth, and that is a heavenly judgment that leads to the Second Coming. And this judgment is the direct parallel of the cleansing of the sanctuary in Daniel 8:14! Considering the events, not to mention the time frame (after the 1,260 years of what can be only papal Roman hegemony), what other sanctuary can be referred to here, other than the heavenly? The last functioning earthly sanctuary was wiped off the map in the first century A.D. Nothing remains but part of a wall. Thus, there's no question that the sanctuary being cleansed in Daniel 8:14 is the sanctuary in heaven. It can be no other, because in this end-time frame the Bible recognizes no other.

When you consider the importance that these two chapters (Daniel 7 and 8) place on this judgment and the cleansing of the sanctuary, it makes sense that the Bible would dedicate almost an entire chapter in the New Testament to the work of Christ as our High Priest in the heavenly sanctuary. The book of Hebrews is unequivocal about Christ's high-priestly ministry in the heavenly sanctuary (Hebrews 7–9). And not only does Hebrews refer to the sanctuary and to Christ's ministry in it, the book gives a clear reference to its cleansing as well:

And almost all things are by the law purged with blood; and without shedding of blood is no remission. It was therefore necessary that the patterns of things in the heavens should be purified with these; but the heavenly things themselves with better sacrifices than these. For Christ is not entered into the holy places made with hands, which are the figures of the true; but into heaven itself, now to appear in the presence of God for us (Hebrews 9:22-24).

Notice in these texts (1) the unequivocal reality of the heavenly sanctuary, (2) the correspondence of the heavenly sanctuary with the earthly type, which is depicted as a pattern "of the things in the heavens," (3) the depiction of Christ doing something in our behalf in the sanctuary, that is, doing something for us even after His death and resurrection, and (4) the need for the heavenly sanctuary to be "purified," or "cleansed" (as many modern translations have it). In fact, the Greek word in Hebrews 9:23 translated as "purified" in the KJV (and as "cleansed" in the NAS and ASV) comes from the same Greek word that the Septuagint used both in Leviticus 16 and in Daniel 8:14 in reference to the cleansing of the sanctuary. Thus, Hebrews here seems to be making a direct reference to what Daniel 8:14 is talking about as well—the cleansing of the heavenly sanctuary. Non-Adventist scholars have seen in Hebrews 9:23 a reference to the Day of Atonement for the heavenly sanctuary. Here are two non-Adventists commenting on Hebrews 9:23. Notice their clear references to the cleansing of the heavenly sanctuary:

> To say "it is necessary that the representations of the heavenly things be cleansed by such rites" (23a) summarizes aspects of Mosaic Law, especially the directive that the sanctuary be cleansed with goat's blood on the Day of Atonement (Lev 16:15-19). . . . The peculiar idea that the heavenly sanctuary might need cleansing (NOTE on 9:23) reflects a view of revelation. The author understands fundamental reality to be heavenly rather than earthly. If the earthly sanctuary is a representation of the heavenly one (8:2, 5), then the laws pertaining to the earthly tent presumably disclose something about the heavenly tent that it represents. One might conclude that the earthly sanctuary was cleansed because its heavenly counterpart also was to be cleansed. Christ did not purify the heavenly sanctuary because he is bound to follow the Levitical pattern; rather the reverse is true. Levitical practice foreshadows Christ's cleansing of the heavenly tent at the turn of the ages (10:1).[13]

The medium for cleansing the affronting defilements from the place of mediation was blood, the repository of the "life" that, once spilled, became a detergent capable of removing the ritual and moral pollution. The author of Hebrews constructs an antithesis in 9:23 that recalls the "lesser to the greater" argument of 9:13-14; just as the new rites involved cleansing the conscience (rather than the surface) of the sinner with a more effective blood, so also the better sanctuary is to be cleansed by the means of better blood as well. . . . Jesus' cleansing of the heavenly sanctum is the ritual enactment of God's promised resolution to "remember sins no more" (Jer. 31:34, cited in Heb. 8:12; 10:15-18).[14]

Thus, unless someone is hopelessly predisposed to the Antiochus interpretation, which limits the events of Daniel to a pre-Christian era, then it is clear (given the historical time-frame) that Daniel 8:14 is talking about the heavenly sanctuary, the same sanctuary depicted in Hebrews, where Christ ministers in our behalf—the sanctuary that, according to the book of Hebrews, must itself be cleansed.

## "WITHIN THE VEIL"

No attack on the pre-Advent judgment would be complete without the mantra "within the veil," taken from this passage in Hebrews:

That by two immutable things, in which it was impossible for God to lie, we might have a strong consolation, who have fled for refuge to lay hold upon the hope set before us: Which hope we have as an anchor of the soul, both sure and stedfast, and which entereth into that *within the veil*; Whither the forerunner is for us entered, even Jesus, made an high priest for ever after the order of Melchisedec (Hebrews 6:18-20, italics supplied).

"Within the veil," Brother Dale, asserts must refer to the veil that separates the first from the second apartment in the heavenly sanctuary. Therefore, according to him, if Christ went "within the veil," He must have entered into the Most Holy Place, the second apartment, right after the Cross and not in 1844 as Adventists teach. He then lists a few verses from Hebrews that he claims buttress his position. How interesting, however, that the verses he quotes (Hebrews 9:8, 12, 24; 10:19, 20) all come from the NIV, which translates the crucial phrase as "Most Holy Place," in contrast, for instance, to the NEB, which translates those same phrases as "sanctuary." As we'll soon see, the NEB is the better translation.

To begin, if one were to read Hebrews cold, that is, without any theological predispositions, the basic message is that Jesus—first as our Sacrifice, and now as our High Priest—has inaugurated a new era in salvation history. All that has come before Him, the entire earthly sanctuary service with its blood, its sacrifices, and its covenant, though instituted by God Himself, has been swept away, replaced by a better sanctuary, by better blood, and by a better covenant (the new covenant). According to Hebrews, the old way was only a shadow, a prefiguring of what Christ—through His death, His resurrection, and now His high priestly ministry in heaven—would accomplish for us. This theme permeates the book of Hebrews, climaxing with these verses:

> *Now of the things which we have spoken this is the sum:* We have such an high priest, who is set on the right hand of the throne of the Majesty in the heavens; A minister of the sanctuary, and of the true tabernacle, which the Lord pitched, and not man. For every high priest is ordained to offer gifts and sacrifices: wherefore it is of necessity that this man have somewhat also to offer. For if he were on earth, he should not be a priest, seeing that there are priests that offer gifts according to the law: Who serve unto the example and shadow of heavenly things, as Moses was admonished of God when he was about to make the tabernacle: for, See, saith he, that thou make all things according to the pattern shewed to thee in the mount. But now hath he obtained a more excellent ministry, by how much also he is the mediator of a better covenant, which was established upon better promises (Hebrews 8:1-6, italics supplied).

What is the sum of the things "which we have spoken" in the first seven chapters of the book? It is the idea that instead of the old covenant priesthood and sanctuary, we have the new covenant priesthood and sanctuary, where Jesus is the High Priest ministering in the "true tabernacle," the sanctuary in heaven. Hebrews compares the old covenant sanctuary service to the new and better one, the one inaugurated by Christ.

The issue is not which apartment Christ went into, or whether the Day of Atonement ritual (as opposed to the daily sacrifice) had been consummated at Christ's ascension to heaven. That's never addressed anywhere because that's not what Hebrews is about, explicitly or implicitly. Hebrews is simply about Christ as our new covenant High Priest ministering in our behalf, making intercession for us (Hebrews 7:25) in the heavenly sanctuary before the Father, doing for us something that the old covenant priesthood and sanctuary service could never do—giving us direct access to God Himself through the intercession of Jesus. The book focuses on the contrast, the comparison, between the old and the new, the earthly and the heavenly, the inferior to the superior, the shadow to the real.

But what about the phrase, "within the veil," which according to Brother Ratzlaff, shows that by the time Hebrews had been written, Christ "had already entered the Most Holy Place of the heavenly sanctuary"[15]?

There's no question that in most, but not all, Old Testament references the phrase "within the veil" refers to the Most Holy Place of the earthly tabernacle. But it's fascinating to see that this phrase is almost always used with certain qualifiers which identify it *specifically* as the second apartment. In other words, "within the veil" itself, left alone, is too ambiguous a phrase for one to assert, dogmatically, that it refers only to the second apartment.

Look at some of these references:

And thou shalt hang up the vail under the taches, that thou mayest bring in *thither within the vail the ark of the testimony*: and *the vail shall divide unto you between the holy place and the most holy.* And thou shalt put the mercy seat upon the ark of the testimony in the most holy place (Exodus 26:33, 34, italics supplied).

And the Lord said unto Moses, Speak unto Aaron thy brother, that he come not at all times into the holy place *within the vail before the mercy seat,* which is upon the ark; that he die not: for I will appear in the cloud upon the mercy seat (Leviticus 16:2, italics supplied).

And he shall take a censer full of burning coals of fire from off the altar before the Lord, and his hands full of sweet incense beaten small, and bring it *within the vail: And he shall put the incense upon the fire before the Lord, that the cloud of the incense may cover the mercy seat that is upon the testimony,* that he die not: And he shall take of the blood of the bullock, and sprinkle it with his finger upon the mercy seat eastward; and before the mercy seat shall he sprinkle of the blood with his finger seven times. Then shall he kill the goat of the sin offering, that is for the people, and bring his blood *within the vail,* and do with that blood as he did with the blood of the bullock, and sprinkle *it upon the mercy seat, and before the mercy seat* (Leviticus 16:12-15, italics supplied).

In each of these cases the phrase "within the vail" doesn't hang loose, without amplification. In each example, it comes with other words, either immediately or later in the text, that show, specifically, what part of the earthly sanctuary was intended, in these cases the Most Holy Place.

Contrast these texts with this one, where the phrase itself "within the vail" is used without specific amplification (as is also the case in Hebrews 6:19):

Therefore thou and thy sons with thee shall keep your priest's office for everything of the altar, and *within the vail;* and ye shall serve: I have given your priest's office unto you as a service of gift: and the stranger that cometh nigh shall be put to death (Numbers 18:7, italics supplied).

The context is important. The Lord told Aaron about his duties regarding the sanctuary; and though the Levites would also have responsibilities regarding the sanctuary, certain things were left only to Aaron and his sons.

In verse 5, talking about Aaron and his sons, the Lord says, "And ye shall keep the charge *of the sanctuary,* and the charge *of the altar:* that there be no wrath any more upon the children of Israel" (Numbers 18:5, italics supplied). Two things are singled out here for their charge: the sanctuary (including, one would assume, all that's in it, because no one else but Aaron and his sons were allowed in) and the altar, that is, the altar of burnt offerings, which stood outside the sanctuary tent itself. Thus, according to verse 5, the sanctuary and the altar were the special charge of Aaron and his sons, the priests.

In verse 6, the Lord talks again about what He said in verse 4, that the Levites would have certain responsibilities. Then in verse 7, shifting back to Aaron and his sons, the Lord repeats what He had said in verse 5, that is, showing the special responsibilities that Aaron and his sons would have as distinct from those of the Levites in general:

Therefore thou and thy sons with thee shall keep your priest's office for everything *of the altar,* and *within the vail;* and ye shall serve: I have given your priest's office unto you as a service of gift: and the stranger that cometh nigh shall be put to death (Numbers 18:7, italics supplied).

Compare this with verse 5, where the Lord is talking specifically to Aaron regarding his duty and the duty of His sons, the priests:

And ye shall keep the charge *of the sanctuary,* and the charge *of the altar:* that there be no wrath any more upon the children of Israel (Numbers 18:5, italics supplied).

See the parallel between the two verses:

| **Verse 5** | | **Verse 7** |
|---|---|---|
| Altar | = | Altar |
| Sanctuary | = | "Within the vail" |

These verses parallel "within the vail" and "the sanctuary." One verse says that Aaron and his sons are in charge of the altar and the sanctuary; the other says that they are in charge of the altar and that which is "within the vail," that is, the sanctuary. Both are talking about the same thing.

Thus, here at least, "within the vail," without all those qualifiers, is clearly a reference to the whole sanctuary, strong evidence that without qualifiers (as in Hebrews 6:19), the phrase "within the vail" refers not to the Most Holy Place but to the entire sanctuary. This idea fits well with the overall theme of Hebrews, which isn't *where* Jesus went in the heavenly sanctuary, but the fact that He *is in there,* ministering in our behalf.

Also, those who argue dogmatically that "within the vail" must mean the Most Holy Place can take little comfort from Hebrews 9:1-3. Here, talking specifically about the earthly sanctuary and the two apartments that composed it, the text reads:

Then verily the first covenant had also ordinances of divine service, and a worldly sanctuary. For there was a tabernacle made; the first, wherein was the candlestick, and the table, and the shewbread; which is called the sanctuary. And after the second veil, the tabernacle which is called the Holiest of all (Hebrews 9:1-3).

These verses are revelatory for a number of reasons.

First, we have here, without ambiguity, a reference to the second apartment *alone*, the Most Holy Place. Verse 3 says, "after the second veil" there is "the Holiest of all," meaning here, of course, the Most Holy Place.

Now, letting the Bible interpret itself and grasping what is sure to help us interpret what isn't so sure, we can see that the author of Hebrews here uses the phrase "after the second veil," in reference to the Most Holy Place, as opposed to the phrase "within the veil." If he wanted to dogmatically assert in Hebrews 6:19 that Jesus was in the second apartment, why didn't he use the same phrase "after the second veil," as he does in 9:3, which without any equivocation points directly to the Most Holy Place? Or why didn't he use the previous language of 6:19 ("within the veil") in 9:3 if that phrase refers to the Most Holy Place—instead of calling it that which was "after the second veil"?

Can one argue that these are merely two different expressions for the same thing?

Perhaps. But the better answer, the one that fits the entire context of Hebrews, is that in Hebrews 6:19 the author was referring to the whole sanctuary where Jesus has entered for us, while in 9:3 the author was pointing to the Most Holy Place alone.

Why is this the better argument?

The Greek word *ta hagia* and its variants occur ten times in the book of Hebrews. The basic meaning of the word is "the holies," basically, "the sanctuary." It's also the word that's used to describe where Jesus is now as our High Priest in heaven; it's also another key that debunks the claim that Hebrews puts Christ in the Most Holy Place of the heavenly sanctuary.

Again, the issue in Hebrews is not which apartment, Holy or Most Holy, Christ entered into, but that He is our High Priest in the heavenly sanctuary. However, in order to answer the dogmatic charge that Hebrews puts Christ in the Most Holy Place just after the Cross, let's see what the Greek says regarding where Christ is.

Look again at Hebrews 9:1-3. The context is clear. The author is describing the earthly sanctuary with its two apartments:

> Then verily the first covenant had also ordinances of divine service, and a worldly sanctuary. For there was a tabernacle made; the first, wherein was the candlestick, and the table, and the shewbread; which is called the sanctuary. And after the second

veil, the tabernacle which is called *the Holiest of all* (Hebrews 9:1-3, italics supplied).

There is no question that in verse 3 the phrase, "the holiest of all" refers to the second apartment of the earthly sanctuary. That's certain. The Greek there uses a unique variant of *ta hagia* that is used nowhere else in the New Testament—*hagia hagion,* which means, "the holy of holies," a clear, nondebatable reference to the second apartment *alone.* Notice the emphasis on "alone"; it gets important later.

Now, in all the other texts where Hebrews uses a variant *of ta hagia,* including those that talk about Jesus' location in heaven, it's revealing that not one uses the phrase *hagia hagion,* "the holy of holies," an unambiguous reference to the Most Holy Place alone. If, as some insist, Hebrews throughout the book absolutely puts Christ in the Most Holy Place immediately following His return to heaven, why does it never use the one phrase which unequivocally, unambiguously means "Most Holy Place" when it describes where Christ is in heaven? Instead it uses variants of *ta hagia* that, in most cases, are referring to the sanctuary as a whole.

Let's proceed to another text that uses a variant of *ta hagia;* in fact, it's the text that first introduces the word in Hebrews:

Now of the things which we have spoken this is the sum: We have such an high priest, who is set on the right hand of the throne of the Majesty in the heavens; A minister of *the sanctuary,* and of the true tabernacle, which the Lord pitched, and not man (Hebrews 8:1, 2, italics supplied).

Here we have another unambiguous use of *ta hagia.* Verse two says that Christ is a minster of "the sanctuary" (from *ta hagia);* the context makes it clear that the author is referring to the whole sanctuary, which he says is "the true tabernacle, which the Lord pitched, and not man." There's no question that the use of "*ta hagia"* here, in its first appearance in the book of Hebrews, is talking about the sanctuary in heaven as a whole, as opposed to any of individual apartments.

The next use is Hebrews 9:1, which reads, "Then verily the first covenant had also ordinances of divine service, and a worldly *sanctuary"* (italics supplied). The phrase "worldly sanctuary" comes also from "*ta hagia"* in another unambiguous reference to the sanctuary as a whole, as opposed to any single apartment, more evidence that the basic meaning of the phrase is the sanctuary itself.

Then there's 9:2, which reads, "For there was a tabernacle made; the first, wherein was the candlestick, and the table, and the shewbread; which is called the *sanctuary*" (italics supplied). Though this is one of the more complicated uses of the word, the context seems a clear reference to the first apartment, the Holy Place, of the earthly sanctuary. Whatever the ambiguity of the word itself (whether the Greek word is neuter plural or feminine singular), the reference to the first apartment is clear.

Then there's 9:3, which we have looked at already, with its unique use of the phrase *"hagia hagion,"* "the holy of holies," unquestionably the second apartment alone.

Next is Hebrews 9:8. Keep the context in mind—the author of Hebrews is contrasting the earthly sanctuary service with the heavenly. After talking about the work of the priest in the Holy Place and the Most Holy Place of the earthly sanctuary, the author writes:

> The Holy Ghost this signifying, that the way into *the holiest of all* was not yet made manifest, while as the first tabernacle was yet standing: Which was a figure for the time then present, in which were offered both gifts and sacrifices, that could not make him that did the service perfect, as pertaining to the conscience; Which stood only in meats and drinks, and divers washings, and carnal ordinances, imposed on them until the time of reformation (Hebrews 9:8-10, italics supplied).

Notice, he's contrasting the earthly service, "the first tabernacle,"[16] which was a "figure for the time then present" with "the time of reformation," that is the new system that Christ has inaugurated through His death, resurrection, and now high-priestly ministry in the heavenly sanctuary. Though translated in the KJV as "the holiest of all," the word is from *ta hagia,* "the holies," or simply the "sanctuary," which, again makes better sense, given the context of comparing the old system to the new. What he's saying is that the way into the heavenly sanctuary (the RSV and the NEB both translate it as "the sanctuary") didn't happen while the earthly, the first tabernacle, was still functioning. Also, if the "Most Holy Place" was meant, why didn't the author use the unambiguous phrase for "holy of holies," that is, *"hagia hagion"*?

The next use is in Hebrews 9:12. Again, follow the flow of thought. We just saw how verses 8-10 contrasted the earthly sanctuary to the heavenly. Verses 11 and 12 parallel the same idea (focus on heavenly/earthly contrast):

> But Christ being come an high priest of good things to come, by a greater and more perfect tabernacle, not made with hands, that is to say, not of this building; Neither by the blood of goats and calves, but by his own blood he entered in once into *the holy place*, having obtained eternal redemption for us (italics supplied).

Again, if the "holy of holies," that is, the second apartment, were meant, why didn't the author use that phrase ("*hagia hagion*") instead of the phrase, "the holies," which means simply, "the sanctuary"? Instead, here's another contrast between the earthly and the heavenly sanctuary, nothing more.

Next is Hebrews 9:24. The verses that precede it are talking about what happened in the earthly sanctuary. Then, the author writes, "For Christ is not entered into *the holy places* made with hands, which are a figure of the true, but into heaven itself, now to appear in the presence of God for us" (Hebrews 9:24, italics supplied). The word is, literally, the "holies," and not *hagia hagion* "the holy of holies." The use of "into heaven itself" shows that the issue here isn't which apartment He's in, but only that's He in the heavenly sanctuary.

Those who argue that Hebrews puts Christ in the "Most Holy Place" immediately following His return to heaven think that they have something with the next verse—Hebrews 9:25. However, that verse works directly against them. In an unambiguous reference to the high priest's Day of Atonement ministry, the text says, "Nor yet that he should offer himself often, as the high priest entereth into *the holy place* every year with the blood of others" (Hebrews 9:25, italics supplied). Now, what's interesting here is that the Greek for "the holy place" is, literally, *ta hagia,* "the holies," the exact phrase used in 9:12, which was a clear reference to the whole sanctuary. But in this case we have a clear reference to "the Most Holy Place," do we not? Thus, if *ta hagia* here means "the Most Holy Place," aren't we justified in saying that's what it means in other verses, where the meaning isn't as unambiguous?

On the surface, that's a good argument. However, that's only the surface argument, and it's based on a faulty premise, which is that this text is referring to the Most Holy Place *alone*. But that's not the case. Instead, the high priest, on the Day of Atonement, went into *both apartments* on the Day of Atonement, not just the Most Holy Place (see Leviticus 16:16-20), which is why Hebrews 9:25, in referring to where the high priest entered, used the phrase for the entire sanctuary (*ta hagia*), as opposed to the phrase for the Most Holy Place alone (*hagia hagion*). He was talking about the *entire* sanctuary, not a single apartment. If he meant only "the Most Holy Place," he would have used the phrase that means only "the Most Holy Place" (*hagia hagion*). But because he meant the entire sanctuary, he used the word that meant the entire sanctuary. Far then from proving their case, this text is more evidence against the claim of those who argue that Hebrews contradicts the Seventh-day Adventist position.

One or two more texts in Hebrews use the phrase. Here's the first: "Having therefore, brethren, boldness to enter *into the holiest* by the blood of Jesus, By a new and living way, which he hath consecrated for us, through the veil, that is to say, his flesh" (Hebrews 10:19, italics supplied). Again, the Greek means simply "the holies" (as opposed to the unambiguous phrase for "the Most Holy Place"); plus the context is, again, a contrast between the old and new system, with the author now saying that we have complete and full access to God in the heavenly sanctuary, as opposed to the limited access the old, earthly one offered the believer.

The final use appears in Hebrews 13:11, a clear reference to the sanctuary; that's why *ta hagia*, as opposed to *hagia hagion*, is used.

What have we seen? Brother Dale takes one phrase, "within the veil," itself somewhat ambiguous, and with it attempts to debunk our entire sanctuary message, despite the powerful evidence of the texts themselves, particularly their use of *ta hagia*, which—far from placing Christ in the Most Holy Place alone—proves that the book of Hebrews simply puts Him in the heavenly sanctuary itself.

It should be noted, too, that scholars have long suggested that the author of Hebrews was influenced by the Septuagint, an ancient Greek version of the Hebrew Bible. In the Septuagint, *ta hagia* is the common term for "the sanctuary," and is never used, even once, in reference to the Most Holy Place alone. This appears to be the same pattern revealed in Hebrews, which isn't surprising, given the influence of the Septuagint on the author of Hebrews. According to one study, of the 109 times *ta hagia* appears in the Septuagint, 106 of those instances refer to the entire sanctuary, while three refer to the first apartment. None refer, ever, to the Most Holy Place.[17]

In short, Brother Dale's assertion that the phrase "within the veil" invalidates our sanctuary theology is, itself invalid. Though the issue in Hebrews isn't which apartment Christ entered, if one insists on dogmatically pushing for one apartment over the other, then the evidence is decidedly *against* the Most Holy Place.

## 457 B.C. AND ALL THAT

Of course, Brother Dale (miming Dr. Ford) assaults the dates 457 B.C., A.D. 27, A.D. 31, and A.D. 34. He doesn't, however, come up with any alternatives, which leads to an interesting and (as we'll see) crucial point.

To begin, the issue of these dates centers around Daniel 9:24-27, a prophecy that Adventists, along with many other Christians, believe points to Jesus Christ. A perusal of the literature, however, shows that most modern commentators (working from premises that often reject the idea of predicative prophecy in the Bible) believe the subject of these verses to be, not Jesus but, . . . you guessed it—Antiochus Epiphanes. However wrong they may be about that, at least they see the link between Daniel 9 and Daniel 8, which they view as referring to Antiochus as well. Antiochus, of course, has nothing to do with either chapter. Daniel 9 is about Jesus, not Antiochus.

And the fact that it's about Jesus adds a crucial element to the question about these dates, an element that critics have to ignore. Des Ford, Dale Ratzlaff, and others all want to debunk 457 B.C.; and that's fine as long as one realizes that by playing with these dates we're tampering with the dates regarding Jesus. As long as one believes that the seventy weeks of Daniel 9 refer to Jesus, one is quite limited in options regarding the starting point of the seventy weeks—and, thus, the 2,300 days. Though we shouldn't be too dogmatic about "proving" the exact dates of Jesus' ministry, Scripture does provide material that can pinpoint the general time frame, and that's crucial for us (as we'll soon see) in responding to attacks on 457 B.C.

Look at the following texts:

> And it came to pass in those days, that there went out a decree from *Caesar Augustus,* that all the world should be taxed. (And this taxing was first made when *Cyrenius* was governor of Syria.) And all went to be taxed, every one into his own city. And Joseph also went up from Galilee, out of the city of Nazareth, into Judaea, unto the

city of David, which is called Bethlehem; (because he was of the house and lineage of David:) To be taxed with Mary his espoused wife, being great with child. And so it was, that, while they were there, the days were accomplished that she should be delivered. And she brought forth her firstborn son, and wrapped him in swaddling clothes, and laid him in a manger; because there was no room for them in the inn (Luke 2:1-7, italics supplied).

Now when Jesus was born in Bethlehem of Judaea in the days of *Herod the king,* behold, there came wise men from the east to Jerusalem (Matthew 2:1, italics supplied).

And he [Joseph] arose, and took the young child and his mother, and came into the land of Israel. But when he heard that *Archelaus* did reign in Judaea in the room of his father Herod, he was afraid to go thither: notwithstanding, being warned of God in a dream, he turned aside into the parts of Galilee (Matthew 2:19-22, italics supplied).

Notice the "secular" figures mentioned in these verses in the context of Christ's birth—Caesar Augustus, Cyrenius the governor of Syria, King Herod, and Herod's son Archelaus. In other words, certain historical figures, some better known than others, some more easily datable than others, are presented here—figures that help give a historical background regarding the time of Christ's birth.

Now in the *fifteenth year* of the reign of *Tiberius Caesar, Pontius Pilate* being governor of Judaea, and *Herod being tetrarch of Galilee,* and his brother *Philip tetrarch of Ituraea* and of the region of Trachonitis, and *Lysanias* the tetrarch of Abilene, *Annas and Caiaphas* being the high priests, the word of God came unto John the son of Zacharias in the wilderness. And he came into all the country about Jordan, preaching the baptism of repentance for the remission of sins (Luke 3:1-3, italics supplied).

Notice, here, too, some of these other historical figures—Tiberius Caesar, Pontius Pilate, Herod, Philip, Annas, Caiaphas—all associated with the time of John the Baptist, who baptized Jesus when Jesus was thirty years old (Luke 3:23; Matthew 3:13-17). We have here, then, other historical personages some of whom can be dated—again with varying degrees of accuracy.

> When the morning was come, all the chief priests and elders of the people took counsel against Jesus to put him to death: And when they had bound him, they led him away, and delivered him to *Pontius Pilate* the governor (Matthew 27:1, 2).

> And as soon as he knew that he belonged unto *Herod's* jurisdiction, he sent him to Herod, who himself also was at Jerusalem at that time (Luke 23:7, italics supplied).

This verse associates more historical figures with Jesus, this time in connection with His death. We haven't even touched the historical figures who appear in the books of Acts which unfolded *after* Christ's death, and which also establish a basic chronological template that helps reveal to us the time that Christ lived and died.

Why is this important? Because we link the seventy weeks of Daniel 9 with the 2,300 days of Daniel 8, and because we believe that the time prophecy of the seventy weeks sets the starting date for the 2,300-day prophecy. And the starting date of the seventy weeks will determine the end point of the 2,300 days, which we put at 1844. Those who attack the 1844 date simply have to show that the date with which we start the seventy weeks—457 B.C.—is wrong. If that's off, even by a year, then the 2,300 days (years) don't end in 1844.

Now many of the books that Brother Dale references deal with this topic, though Brother Dale—repeating the arguments from Dr. Ford—ignores their defenses of the date. I don't want to repeat those defenses; plenty of material is out there. I want to take a somewhat different approach, one that centers around the chronological historicity of Christ, because as both Sacrifice (the seventy-week prophecy) and High Priest (the 2,300-day prophecy) He is at the center. We can work back from when Jesus lived and died, and from that time-frame establish the beginning of the seventy-week prophecy, which, by default, gives us the end of the 2,300 days.

Daniel 9:25 reads, "Know therefore and understand, that from the going forth of the commandment to restore and to build Jerusalem unto the Messiah the Prince shall be. . . ." Thus, the date we're looking for deals with the command to "restore and rebuild Jerusalem," obviously after the city had been destroyed by the Babylonians. Using the Reformation principle of *sola scriptura*, we need to find something in the Bible that establishes the date.

Various dates have been given for this decree, including 538 B.C., 520 B.C., 457 B.C., 458 B.C., and 444 B.C. Much has been written by our scholars on the historical background to these dates.[18] However, let's tackle the issue from a different angle.

Suppose someone were to accept 538 B.C. as the starting point for the seventy weeks. From the command to restore and rebuild Jerusalem (538 B.C.) until the fulfillment of all the events in the prophecy (the first advent of Jesus, His death, the confirming of the covenant, etc.) would be 490 years. If we use 538 B.C. as the starting point, 490 years reaches to. . . what? 48 B.C. Now, given what we know historically about Jesus and the historical events surrounding His life and ministry, does anyone believe that 48 B.C. fits within the general time frame of Christ's earthly ministry? Of course not.

It's the same with 520 B.C. If we use that date, the seventy weeks end in 30 B.C., a date that in no way fits with the time that Jesus lived and died.

However, if we go with 457 B.C., the seventh year of the reign of Artaxerxes (see Ezra 7:8-26), the numbers come right to the time of Christ, that is, to 27–34 A.D. And though we can't be overly dogmatic about proving those exact dates from historical sources, we certainly can be dogmatic about 457 B.C., in contrast to the other dates looked at so far, as being the only starting point that could possibly bring us to "Messiah the Prince." Also, for what it's worth, while reading A. Rupert Hall's famous biography of Isaac Newton, I came across this sentence: "Who cares whether Newton was correct in maintaining that the prophecy of the seventy weeks in the book of Daniel referred to the interval of 490 years after Ezra's leading the Jews from Babylon back to Jerusalem (457 B.C.) to the Crucifixion in A.D. 33/34."[19] Though this hardly proves our position is correct, it proves that we aren't the only ones to have held it.

This decree in 457 B.C. was given by Artaxerxes I, and it's clear that not only the Jews, but their enemies, understood that whatever else the decree entailed, it included the rebuilding of the city. In Ezra 4:7-13 (the events in Ezra are not in chronological order), a group of Persian officers wrote to King Artaxerxes, complaining about the Jews rebuilding Jerusalem. In the letter they stated two important points: (1) that the city was being rebuilt (Ezra 4:12), and (2) that the Jews who were rebuilding it had come there because of the king. Said the letter, "Be it known unto the king, *that the Jews which came up from thee to us* are come unto Jerusalem, *building the rebellious and the bad city,* and have set up the walls thereof, and joined the foundations" (verse 12, italics supplied). In other words, the Jews who were rebuilding the city had come there because of King Artaxerxes, and the only decree issued by the king that sent the Jews back to Jerusalem (at least the only such decree that appears in the Bible) was in the seventh year of his reign, a date that can be established as 457 B.C.

Could one argue that it was another decree, other than the one in Ezra 7, which wasn't mentioned in the Bible? One could, but at what cost? Here we have the most powerful prophecy in the Bible, one giving us the dates of Jesus the Messiah hundreds of years in advance—*and yet the Bible itself doesn't give us the starting point?* That's hardly credible. If we work on the *sola scriptura* principle, that the Bible interprets itself, we must believe that the Bible would provide a solid and trustworthy starting point for this crucial prophecy (as well as for the 2,300 days). And it does, with the decree issued by Artaxerxes in the seventh year of his reign, as shown in Ezra 7.

What about 445 B.C. as a starting point for the seventy weeks? If we do the numbers, the seventy weeks would end in 45 A.D., and although that's better than some other dates, who believes that Jesus—"cut off" in the midst of the last week—was killed about 42 A.D.?

Now, there's the last date proposed as an alternative to 457 B.C.—458 B.C. This amounts to a difference of six months. The following are a few quotes from non-Adventist sources, all putting the seventh year of Artaxerxes as 458 B.C. Though most are writing in another context, notice the date they give for the return of Ezra to Jerusalem:

> Many scholars decided in favor of Artaxerxes I, and so fix the seventh year of Artaxerxes in Ezra 7 as 458. . . .[20]

> A straightforward reading of the biblical texts places Ezra's arrival in Judah in 458 BCE. . . . [21]

> According to the biblical sources both [Ezra and Nehemiah] were active in the time of Artaxerxes I Longimanus. The date of Ezra's coming to Jerusalem in the seventh year of the king's rule would then be 458 B.C.[22]

In an article attacking the 457 B.C. date as the starting point of the seventy weeks, Desmond Ford wrote the following:

> But there is a final problem: even those scholars who believe Ezra 4 may refer to the time of Ezra and the decree of Ezra 7 do not accept the 457 B.C. date for the decree! The date most universally accepted is 458 B.C., and in the spring—certainly not October 22. Sadly, 2,300 years from that date does not culminate in 1844.[23]

No—it culminates in 1843! One year off (not even a full year, either). Thus, even if we use 458 B.C., this places the heavenly, pre-Advent judgment (both in Daniel 7 and 8) in 1843, as opposed to 1844. The fact is, though, enough scholarly work has been done to show that 457 is, indeed, the better of the two dates.[24]

What's fascinating, too, is that while both Brother Dale and Des Ford attack 457 B.C., they don't give an alternative date. In the article slashing at 457 B.C., Ford talks about the decree of Cyrus being the better one to fulfill the prophecy than the decree of Artaxerxes in 457 B.C. Interestingly enough, he doesn't pursue that thought. He just throws it out[25] as part of his attempted debunking of 1844 and then goes on. Why? Could it be because he knows that the decree of Cyrus cannot possibly work—that is, if one believes that the seventy weeks are a reference to Jesus—because that starting point would put the time of Christ decades before He lived on earth. Dr. Ford, apparently, didn't want to pursue this line of thought any further than he took it. He simply wanted to attack our belief and then move on. One can hardly blame him.

Brother Ratzlaff goes on to attack 27 A.D., 31 A.D., and 34 A.D. However, for our immediate purposes, these arguments aren't important. What's crucial is the starting date of the seventy weeks, a date tied directly to Christ. And, as we've seen, we're on solid ground here.

In the end, those who attack 457 B.C. as the starting date for the seventy weeks have the onus on them of providing another date from Scripture, a date that would put the seventy weeks in a time that fits the time of Jesus, a date that also establishes the starting point of the 2,300-year prophecy. Jesus' life and ministry form "borders" that severely limit the options regarding which date one can use for the starting point of the prophecy. Thus Jesus Himself provides us with the foundation for the 2,300-year prophecy. You can't tamper with one and not tamper with the other.

## DAY-YEAR PRINCIPLE: HERE WE GO AGAIN

To this day, I still hear opponents *within the church* attack the day-year principle. Considering the evidence published *within the church* defending it, these attacks are the theological equivalent of an assault on the round-earth paradigm in favor of the flat-earth one. Again, Brother Dale's error in this regard could be excused as lack of information, because he's been out of the loop for so long. But others within the church, who have had access to our best defenses of the day-year principle, continue the assault even though, interestingly enough, they avoid dealing directly with the church's best defenses of the teaching—Dr. Bill Shea's work in *Selected Studies on Prophetic Interpretation*.[26] Though loudly and brashly denying the principle, they never (at least as far as I have seen) address the arguments for it. Opponents make broad statements against the idea, and then flee. Considering the evidence not only for the day-year principle in general but for its application in Daniel 7, 8, and 9 in particular, I can hardly blame them.

I do not intend to reiterate all the defenses. To know more, read Dr. Shea. Ironically enough, one of the best defenses of the day-year principle is found in the appendix of Des Ford's book, *Daniel*.[27] Obviously, he now rejects all that he wrote back then. It's hard to imagine how anyone, after reading Dr. Shea's material (and Ford's, for that matter), could deny the day-year principle on *rational* grounds (emotional grounds, that's another story altogether). Instead of any exhaustive defense, such as Dr. Shea has done, I will touch on a few examples that are enough, I believe, to prove how hollow the attacks on the day-year principle have so far been.

First, there's Daniel 9:24-27. If you interpret the time element literally, you have seventy weeks (about a year and four months) from the command to restore and rebuild Jerusalem unto "the Messiah the Prince," Jesus of Nazareth, who lived in the first century A.D. That's impossible, of course, at least with any of the commonly proposed starting dates, which are all centuries prior to Christ. On the other hand, the day-year principle turns the seventy weeks into almost half a millennium and places "the Messiah the Prince" in the time period in which Jesus lived, something that doesn't happen if the time frame is interpreted literally. Thus, the Messiahship of Jesus proves the validity of the day-year principle. Not a bad foundation, to be sure.

The big argument against this, one that Dr. Ford now uses, is that the phrase in Daniel 9:24, "seventy weeks," really means "seventy weeks of years." If you have seventy "weeks," and each of those weeks is a "week of years," (seven years), then you arrive at 490 years without the day-year principle. Hence, the argument goes, we can arrive at the time of Jesus without the day-year principle.

Numerous problems come with this approach. To begin, everywhere else in the Bible where the word translated "weeks" in Daniel 9:24-27 is used and vocalized as it is in Daniel 9:24-27 it always means "weeks" and not "weeks of years," or "sevens." In that specific form and specific vocalization, it's never translated as anything but "weeks." Why, suddenly, in Daniel 9:24-27 is the meaning changed to something different than the way the word is used everywhere else?

In fact, the same form of the word appears in Daniel 10:2, 3—"In those days I Daniel was mourning three full weeks. I ate no pleasant bread, neither came flesh nor wine in my mouth, neither did I anoint myself at all, till three whole weeks were fulfilled." In both places, the word is "weeks," the same word used in Daniel 9:24-27, and it is translated accurately as "weeks," not "weeks of" anything. Also in both places, the Hebrew phrase translated "three full weeks" is literally "three weeks days." Some have tried to argue (rather sophistically) that it means "three weeks of days," and placing that phrasing in parallel to Daniel 9, which—they argue—because it doesn't have the phrase "of days" following "weeks," must therefore mean "weeks of years."

There are a few blatant problems with that assumption, the first being that the Hebrew word for "weeks" appears in 10:2, 3 in the *absolute* state, that is, it simply means "weeks," not "weeks *of*" anything. Hebrew nouns appear in a special form (construct state) for the genitive case ("house *of* something," as opposed to just "house"), and "weeks" in Daniel 10:2, 3 is definitely not in the construct state. It's not "weeks *of*" anything, but simply "weeks." Therefore, the attempted parallel breaks down, right from the start, on immovable grammatical grounds.

Meanwhile, in biblical Hebrew, time units such as months and years are sometimes followed by the word "days" as an idiomatic expression for "full" or "complete" units (see Genesis 41:1; 29:14). That's all it means, and that's all that's meant in Daniel 10:2, 3. The jump, therefore, from "three full weeks," (Daniel 10:2, 3) to "weeks of years" in Daniel 9:24-27 is a leap in the dark.

"Thus," writes Shea, "the Hebrew expression in Daniel 10:2, 3, namely 'three weeks days,' means, according to this idiom, 'three full weeks,' or 'three whole weeks.' Linguistically this idiom prevents the conclusion from being drawn that 'weeks of days' in contrast to 'weeks of years' is implied in this passage."[28]

One final point. Let's assume there were some linguistic grounds for the translation "weeks of years" in Daniel 9:24-27. Each "week" then would be a "week of years," meaning that each week stood for seven years. How interesting that with the day-year principle, each week stands for seven years as well. In other words, inherent in the idea of a "week of years" is the day-year principle itself. If someone were rationally looking for evidence for the principle, one could find it within the notion of "weeks of years," a scholarly concoction devised to debunk the day-year principle. However, because the day-year principle is so ingrained in the prophecy—so necessary for the prophecy to make sense—something designed to dismiss the principle obliquely supports it!

Now, because the day-year principle is requisite for the seventy weeks and because the seventy weeks are "cut off" from (are part of) the 2,300 days, doesn't it make sense that the 2,300 days would also demand the day-year principle? Of course. If fact, logic demands it, because there's no way that 490 years could be part of, or cut off from, a literal 2,300 days, which is just over six years. The only way to make sense of the relationship between the two prophecies is for the day-year principle to be applied to the 2,300 days as well.

Meanwhile, there's internal evidence within the 2,300 days that it must be understood in terms of the day-year principle. To show this point, I repeat a few paragraphs from an earlier section of this book that was dealing with the question asked in Daniel 8:13, leading to the response in verse 14 that the sanctuary will be cleansed:

> This point can be seen especially in the question that is asked in verse 13: "Then I heard one saint speaking, and another saint said unto that certain saint which spake, How long shall be the vision *concerning* the daily sacrifice, and the transgression of desolation, to give both the sanctuary and the host to be trodden under foot?"
>
> What's crucial is that the word "concerning" does not appear in the Hebrew, nor does Hebrew grammar allow for it. Thus the question isn't just about the activity of the little horn. Instead, the question is about everything depicted in the chapter, which includes the vision about the ram and the goat (Media-Persia and Greece) as well as the activity of the little horn (pagan and papal Rome). A literal translation would read, "How long the vision, the daily, and

the transgression of desolation to give the sanctuary and the host a trampling." In other words, the question lists the things that happened in the vision. In fact, the word for "vision" in verse 13 is *hazon*, which deals with the ram and the goat, that is, Media-Persia and Greece (see the next chapter).

The question, then, could be paraphrased like this, *How long will all these things, from the rise of Media-Persia, the rise of Greece, and finally to Rome's attack on Christ's heavenly ministry, be allowed to go on?*

The point should be obvious: The 2,300 days must cover all the events depicted in the vision of Daniel 8, that is, Media-Persia, Greece, Rome, and the sanctuary cleansed. A literal 2,300 days doesn't even begin to cover one of those kingdoms, much less all. On the other hand, with the day-year principle, the problem is instantly solved. Twenty-three hundred years, not a little more than six years, cover the events in question. In short, the prophecy itself demands the day-year principle.

Likewise, Daniel 7 has built within it the need for the year-day principle. Again, I repeat something from an earlier section in this book, this time in the context of the little-horn power that is part of the fourth beast:

Suffice it to say this much: The little-horn power arises directly out of pagan Rome, which met its demise (as *pagan* Rome) about the fifth or sixth century A.D. Out of it arises this little-horn power, which persecutes the saints for 1,260 "days" (Daniel 7:23-25). After this persecution comes a judgment in heaven that leads to the establishment of God's final kingdom (verses 26, 27).

Now, either the time frame is literal (three and one-half actual years) or it's prophetic (1,260 actual years). Which option works best?

Amid all the prophetic symbols of Daniel 7 (winged lions and leopards, a beast with iron teeth, a horn that has eyes and a mouth), we find a time prophecy depicting the activity of a horn that has a mouth and eyes. If one takes the time frame as a literal three and one-half years (even though it appears amid all these symbols), then one of two options are possible.

First, the persecution was put on hold for at least 1,500 years— remember, the little horn arises after the demise of pagan Rome, which is fifth to sixth century A.D. Meanwhile, the judgment that follows the

1,260 days of persecution ends with the second coming of Christ, which is now at least into the twenty-first century. A major gap, therefore, must exist between the time the little horn arises (sixth century A.D.) and the 1,260 days of persecution that come right before the final judgment, which leads to the Second Coming. Under this scenario, a persecuting power arises out of pagan Rome, *but that persecution doesn't begin for at least 1,500 years and counting?* Remember, we're already in the twenty-first century, and God's kingdom isn't here yet, and it arises after the literal 1,260 days of persecution. That position is possible, but it's not plausible. Besides, nothing in the text indicates that this persecution is put off until the end; all the characteristics of the little horn appear to apply it in total.

The other option is that because these characteristics seem to apply in total to the little horn, with no indication of a delay, then the three and one-half years of persecution should have started early in the little horn's career. This means they must have ended about 1,500 years ago, around the fifth to sixth centuries A.D., 1,260 days after they started. If so, then the judgment that follows has been in session for almost a millennium and a half. This position is likewise possible, but rather untenable, especially for those who mock the Adventist view of the 1844 judgment, saying it's silly for a judgment to be going on for so long, that is, since 1844.

In short, a literal interpretation of Daniel 7:25, which makes the persecution by the little-horn power only three and one-half literal years, is improbable to the point of nonsense.

If, however, the day-year principle is applied to the time prophecy, these problems vanish.

Evidence for the day-year principle abounds in Scripture. Genesis itself is a good start. In what could be called the Bible's first time prophecy, a hint of the principle appears. In the context of the coming Flood, the Lord said, "My spirit shall not always strive with man, for that he also *is* flesh: yet his *days* shall be an hundred and twenty *years*" (Genesis 6:3, italics supplied). See the link, days-years? Though these are only idiomatic expressions, the link between days and years is there.

There's more: "And all the *days* of Cainan were nine hundred and ten *years*," (Genesis 5:14, italics supplied). "And all the *days* of Enoch were three hundred sixty and five *years*" (Genesis 5:23, italics supplied). "And all the *days* of Noah were nine hundred and fifty *years*" (Genesis 9:29, italics supplied). Of itself, this formula (found numerous times in the early pages of the Bible), hardly proves the day-year principle, but it certainly provides at least hints of a link between days and years.

Of course, there's the familiar verse, Numbers 14:34, which by itself wouldn't prove the day-year principle, but together with other evidence unquestionably helps support the idea: "After the number of the days in which ye searched the land, even *forty days, each day for a year,* shall ye bear your iniquities, *even forty years,* and ye shall know my breach of promise" (italics supplied). The following familiar verses don't hurt our case either: "For I have laid upon thee the *years* of their iniquity, *according to the number of the days,* three hundred and ninety days: so shalt thou bear the iniquity of the house of Israel. And when thou hast accomplished them, lie again on thy right side, and thou shalt bear the iniquity of the house of Judah forty days: *I have appointed thee each day for a year*" (Ezekiel 4:5, 6, italics supplied).

Meanwhile, in Hebrew poetry days are used in parallel to years, showing a semantic link between the two time periods:

"Are thy *days* as the days of man?
are thy *years* as man's days" (Job 10:5, italics supplied).

"*Days* should speak,
and multitude of *years* should teach wisdom" (Job 32:7, italics supplied).

"I have considered the *days* of old,
the *years* of ancient times" (Psalm 77:5).

Then there are texts where although the word is translated "days," the obvious meaning is "years." In the context of the Passover, which was kept once a year, Exodus 13:10 reads (in the KJV): "Thou shalt therefore keep this ordinance in his season from *year to year,*" even though the phrase "year to year" is from the literal Hebrew phrase, "from days to days."

Once a year Hannah took the garments she had made for young Samuel to the temple: "Moreover his mother made him a little coat, and brought it to him *from year to year,* when she came up with her husband to offer the *yearly* sacrifice" (1 Samuel 2:19, italics supplied). In Hebrew, from "year to year" is literally, "from days to days." Likewise, "yearly" is literally, "the days." Again, though these are only idiomatic expressions, they do show a definite semantic link between the idea of days and years.

Then, of course, there's that pesky little problem found in Daniel 8, where the prophet was told that the vision was for the "end" (Daniel 8:17, 19). Hard to explain if the 2,300 days, which began in the time of Media-Persia, were only a literal six years. In contrast, the day-year principle solves that dilemma quite nicely.

We don't even need to get into the fact that the time prophecies in Daniel 7 and 8—immersed as they are in prophetic symbols of goats and winged lions (themselves a hint that a literal interpretation of the time prophecies is not meant)—are expressed in uncommon ways of depicting literal time. For example, the phrase "2300 evenings and mornings" isn't how the Bible would normally depict a period of about six years and four months. Why? The reason could be that—coming amid symbolic prophecies—symbolic time, not literal time, was meant.

Also, for what it's worth, the day-year principle is hardly an Adventist concoction. It has been recognized and used by both Jewish and Christian exegetes hundreds of years before Adventism ever arose, and these exegetes even applied the principle to the same prophecies that we do. Though this doesn't prove the truth of the day-year principle, it certainly proves that others, long before William Miller or Ellen and James White, saw in the Bible evidence for the principle, and thus it's not merely some Adventist or Millerite concoction.

There's much more we haven't touched on (read Dr. Shea or even Dr. Ford's *Daniel,* for more than enough evidence proving the validity of our use of the day-year principle). But the point's more than obvious: In light of all the linguistic, theological, and historical evidence in favor of the day-year principle, the burden of proof rests, not on those who believe in the principle, but on those who deny it—despite the evidence.

## CONCLUSION

Now, let's pull together a few of the elements in the past few chapters and show how we arrive at the date of 1844 as the end point of the 2,300-year prophecy of Daniel 8:14.

1. Review the charts that present the parallels between Daniel 2, 7, and 8. See how the judgment scene in Daniel 7, the judgment that leads to the second coming of Christ and the end of this world as we know it, is the same thing as the cleansing of the sanctuary in Daniel 8.

2. Look at the charts and see how the judgment in Daniel 7 and the cleansing of the sanctuary in Daniel 8 occur after the "times, time and dividing of time" (Daniel 7:25); that is, sometime after the late eighteenth or early nineteenth centuries.

3. Notice, too, that Daniel 2 consists of a dream/vision and a complete interpretation of that dream/vision. Daniel 7 consists of a dream/vision and a complete interpretation of that dream/vision. Daniel 8, in contrast, has a dream/vision but only a partial explanation of that dream/vision; the *mareh* of the 2,300 days is the only part not explained. Daniel 9 has no dream, no vision, just an explanation—and, as we have seen above, it is an explanation of the *mareh*, the vision of the evenings and the mornings that Daniel 8 doesn't interpret.

4. We saw, too, how the seventy weeks were cut off from the 2,300 days. Thus we have two time prophecies here, the shorter seventy weeks, and the longer 2,300 days, with the shorter one being cut off from the longer (after all, it couldn't be the other way around, could it?):

**seventy weeks**

_____

**2,300 days**

_____

5. We have seen, too, that of all the dates often proposed for the decree to rebuild Jerusalem and thus the beginning of the seventy weeks and the 2,300 days, the ministry of Jesus Himself establishes 457/458 B.C. as the only viable one. The prophecy is as firm as Christ Himself.

**seventy weeks**
**457** B.C._____A.D. **34**

6. Thus, with the seventy weeks beginning in 457 B.C, and being "cut off" from the 2,300 days (see *1844 Made Simple* for an explanation why it has to be cut off from the beginning, not the end of the 2,300 days), we come to A.D. 1844.

**2,300 years**
**457** B.C._____A.D. **1844**

Do the math. Add 2,300 to -457 and you come to 1843. Add one year to adjust for the year difference between a regular number line and a calendar, and you get 1844. And, surprise of surprises, the date comes out sometime after the 1,260-year period depicted in Daniel 7.

That's all it takes. It's as solid as world history, as solid as Christ, as solid as the math itself.

Now, let's wrap this up.

In the last three chapters we have examined one section alone ("A Biblical Evaluation") of Brother Dale's attack on the investigative judgment, in which he claims to show "a few, clear Bible references" that prove "beyond the shadow of a doubt" not only that the pre-Advent judgment is wrong, but that it is contrary to Scripture "at almost every point."

Again, in Brother Dale's 380-page book against the investigative judgment, only fifteen pages are what he calls "a biblical evaluation." And we've just looked at that evaluation closely. The evidence, I believe, speaks for itself.

Now, as I emphasized earlier, if we can't prove the pre-Advent judgment from the Bible, then there's no need to worry about defending Ellen White and her gift. If the judgment is an error, so is her ministry.

But if the judgment is wrong, Brother Dale needs better evidence than his fifteen-page "biblical evaluation," which is nothing but stale arguments from Dr. Ford. The thought keeps going through my mind: *Is this the best that the critics can do—simply reviving the same old charges against it, charges that have been more than answered?* In all sincerity, I have to say that the continued weakness and shallowness of the same old attacks, as well the entrenched refusal of our critics to confront the *Daniel and Revelation Committee* books, continues to affirm my belief in the truth of the 1844 pre-Advent judgment.

Recently, a retired church scholar wrote a long diatribe against the pre-Advent judgment that consisted of the same old arguments, including the mandatory attack on the day-year principle ("There is no Bible basis whatever for this so-called principle"[29]) as well as on the Daniel and Revelation Committee books, calling them, among other things, "the ultimate exercise in obscurantism posing as the highest level of scholarship Adventists have to offer!"[30] Yet in common with other critics, including Brother Dale, he never dealt with the specific arguments in the volumes. He just lambasted them and moved on. I don't blame him.

We've looked at Brother Dale's "biblical evaluation" of the judgment. It fails, miserably. Does this failure prove that the judgment is true? Of course not. It proves only that one of the church's vociferous critics has been unable to build a solid case, on biblical grounds, against the 1844 pre-Advent judgment. If he could, his attack on Ellen White would carry some weight (indeed, it would be enough to sink her). His big charge, that she supported a false teaching, is undermined because he can't prove that the teaching itself, the pre-Advent judgment, is false.

And yet, as weak as this attack has been, the next one we'll look at—his charge that the pre-Advent judgment is anti-gospel—is even weaker.

---

[1] Desmond Ford, *1844, The Day of Atonement, and the Investigative Judgment,* (Euangelion Press, Castlebury, FL) 1980.

[2] *CDSDA*, p. 175.

[3] *Symposium On Daniel*, Frank Holbrook, editor (Biblical Research Institute, Silver Spring, MD) 1986, pp. 378–426.

[4] *Ibid.*, p. 221.

[5] After *1844 Made Simple* was published, I got a few letters and phone calls from people who, using a *Strong's Concordance*, said that, according to *Strong's*, the word for "vision" at the end of Daniel 9:23 was *hazon*, not *mareh*. I checked; they're right, but the concordance is wrong. The word is *mareh*, not *hazon*. A concordance is, after all, just that, a concordance. It's hardly infallible.

[6] *Daniel*, Art Scroll Tanach Series (Mesorah Publications, Brooklyn, NY) 1988, p. 258.

[7] *CDSDA*, p 175.

[8] *Ibid.*

[9] *Ibid.*, p. 168.

[10] *Symposium on Daniel*, p. 431.

[11] Angel Rodriguez, "The Sanctuary and Its Cleansing," Supplement to the *Adventist Review* (General Conference of SDA, January, 1994), p. 9.

[12] *CDSDA*, p. 177.

[13] Craig R. Koester, *Hebrews,* The Anchor Bible Series (Doubleday, New York, NY) 2001, p. 427.

[14] David A. DeSilva, *Perseverance in Gratitude* (William B. Eerdmans Publishing Company, Grand Rapids, MI) 2000, pp. 312, 313.

[15] *CDSDA*, p. 172.

[16] The phrase, "the first tabernacle," appears in both Hebrews 9:6 and 9:8 in a manner that has caused some understandable confusion. In 9:6, it's an obvious reference to the Holy Place, the first apartment, of the earthly sanctuary. In 9:8, however, the meaning must shift, and it means the entire sanctuary, the earthly one. Otherwise, the text becomes nonsensical. In verse 6, the phrase is being used in a spatial context, denoting *the place* where the priest ministered. In verse 8, it's dealing with the element of *time*, depicting contrast between one dispensation and another. Non-Adventist scholars have noted this shift in the meaning of the phrase as well. To read it otherwise, particularly as do those who insist the text places Christ in the Most Holy of the heavenly sanctuary, would be to read it like this: "The Holy Ghost this signifying, that the way into the Most Holy Place [of the heavenly sanctuary] was not yet made manifest while the holy place [of the earthly sanctuary] was still standing," which, of course, makes no sense.

[17] Carl Coesart, "A Study of *Ta Hagia* in the LXX, Pseudepigrapha, Philo, and Josephus, and its Implications in Hebrews." M.A. thesis, Nazarene Theological Seminary, 2000.

[18] See for instance, *70 Weeks, Leviticus, Nature of Prophecy*, Frank Holbrook, ed. "Commencement Date for the Seventy-Week Prophecy," Arthur J. Ferch (Biblical Research Institute, Washington, DC) 1986, pp. 64–74.

[19] A. Rupert Hall, *Isaac Newton: Adventurer in Thought* (Cambridge University Press, Cambridge) 1992, p. 372.

[20] Otto Eissfelt, *The Old Testament: An Introduction* (Harper and Row, New York, NY) 1965, p. 533.

[21] Norman Gottwald, *The Hebrew Bible: A Socio-Literary Introduction* (Fortress Press, Philadelphia, PA) 1985, p. 435.

[22] S. Talmon, "Ezra and Nehemiah," *IDB Sup,* p. 320.

[23] *Good News Unlimited* (November, 1990) p. 6.

[24] For an entire book on the subject see, Siegfried Horn, Lynn Wood, *The Chronology of Ezra 7* (Review and Herald Publishing Association, Washington, DC) 1953.

[25] *Good News Unlimited,* p. 6.

[26] William Shea, *Selected Studies on Prophetic Interpretation* (General Conference of Seventh-day Adventists, Washington, DC) 1982.

[27] Desmond Ford, *Daniel* (Southern Publishing, Association; Nashville, TN) 1978, Appendix f.

[28] *Ibid.,* p. 76.

[29] http://www.jesusinstituteforum.org/AssetOrLiability.html

[30] *Ibid.*

CHAPTER SIX

# THE

# GOSPEL

## AND THE

# JUDGMENT

My wife, raised in the Adventist Church, once described how, as a child, she had been taught the investigative judgment.

"Well," she said, her voice laced with sarcasm, "they tell you that the judgment is going on in heaven right now, and at any moment your name can come up. And when it does, if you're not perfect (you're at the movies, or something like that), then your name is blotted out of the book of life, and you are forever lost. The only problem is, you don't know that your name has been blotted out, and so you continue trying to be perfect. But it's too late; your probation has closed, and so you must, in the end, face the second death."

Good news, huh?

With such an understanding of the judgment, it's no wonder that some people have entirely abandoned either the doctrine or the Seventh-day Adventist Church which teaches it. Here's where I can, in fact, have some sympathy for Brother Dale. All through the book he expressed what has been (and remains) a problem for many Adventists: harmonizing the judgment and the gospel. This motif appears from the beginning to the end of *CDSDA*, shedding light on, among other things, the psychology of Brother Dale's departure.

For example, in a section titled, "About the author," the book says that Brother Dale "became convinced that this doctrine [the pre-Advent judgment] could not be supported by Scripture, was contrary to clear biblical teaching, and undermined the new covenant gospel of grace."[1]

In the foreword to the book, non-Adventist writer, Kenneth Samples, founder and president of Augustine Fellowship Study Center, says, "I agree with Mr. Ratzlaff that the doctrine of the investigative judgment is antithetical to the biblical gospel. It seems to be clearly incompatible with the doctrine of justification by grace alone, through faith alone, on the account of Christ alone."[2]

Echoing my wife's concern about the judgment, Brother Dale writes: "What if my name would come up when I was having fun playing volleyball? What if my name would come up when I was purchasing new clothes? What if my name would come up when I was focused on earning a livelihood? What if my name would come up in judgment when I had an impure thought? Or, worse yet, had my name already come up? Perhaps my doom was already sealed?"[3]

He writes, too: "I thank God that the gospel is now being taught in some SDA churches. However, the investigative judgment continues to be taught, even at official levels, and the two do not mix."[4] "The SDA teaching of the investigative judgment is a serious theological error, a blatant perversion of the gospel."[5]

He appeals to the church leadership: "Why not cut out the 'sliver' of the cleansing of the heavenly sanctuary and the investigative judgment, *even if* it hurts and the costs are high? Why not determine to be true to the new covenant gospel of grace and the word of God *alone?*"[6] Of course, for Brother Dale, that would mean forgetting about the seventh-day Sabbath as well, but that's another book.

"What a contrast there is," he writes, "between living under the investigative judgment and living under the joyous good news of acquittal in Christ proclaimed in the Epistles of the New Testament!"[7]

However sincere Brother Dale may be in his criticism, and however accurately he may be portraying the dilemma that many people within the church have faced, or still face, his words are a prime example of what I call "folk Adventism"—popular but *false* conceptions about our doctrines. If the Adventist Church really does *teach* what he says it does, then it should *do* what he says, and that is—get rid of the pre-Advent judgment, because any doctrine that goes contrary to the gospel should be abandoned.

Yet the problem isn't with the doctrine itself but with a *misunderstanding* of the doctrine, and that's a crucial distinction. In the same way that some people have been turned off of Christianity because of the poor way Christians have sometimes expressed their faith, many have been turned off of the pre-Advent judgment because of the poor way it has been presented in our pulpits and classrooms. But just as the uncharitable actions of Christians don't take away the truth of Christianity, the poor way Adventists have taught the judgment doesn't take away the truth of the judgment. A lousy recital of Beethoven's *Ninth Symphony* doesn't negate the beauty of the original score.

In fact, far from negating the gospel, the pre-Advent judgment is its climatic denouement. The judgment is the culmination of the Cross, the climax of the good news. The judgment doesn't contradict the Cross; it actually helps us better understand the Cross and what Christ accomplished there for us.

Think about this: If you were a Jew living in ancient Israel during the wilderness wanderings, you would learn about the plan of salvation from the portable tabernacle, for here is where the gospel was presented to Israel in types. Now, suppose your understanding of the plan of salvation was limited only to the death of the animal. You knew only the part of the service that centered around the sacrifice. If nothing else were explained to you—such as the ministry of the priesthood involving the blood of the slain animal in the sanctuary—would you not have a more limited understanding of the plan of salvation than someone who comprehended not only the death of the animal but the ministry in the tabernacle with that animal's blood—particularly the ministry on the Day of Atonement, when the high priest once a year went into the Most Holy Place to perform the work of cleansing the sanctuary? Who would have a larger grasp of salvation, the one whose focus, knowledge, and interest ended with the death of the animal (symbolic of the Cross), or the one whose understanding encompassed the entire sanctuary ritual, starting with the death of the animal and culminating with the Day of Atonement, when the sanctuary itself was cleansed by the blood of that slain animal (symbolic of the judgment)?

The answer is obvious. In the same way, those whose understanding of the plan of salvation is limited only to the Cross, without all that happens afterward, including the judgment, have a truncated view of the Cross. You can't fully understand the death of the animal without understanding the service that followed it; in the same way, you can't fully understand the Cross without understanding the ministry that follows it, and that includes the judgment, as typified by the Day of Atonement ritual.

Think about this too: Was there any tension, much less contradiction, between the death of the animal (which symbolized the Cross) and the ministry of the high priest in the Most Holy Place on the Day of Atonement (which symbolized the judgment)? Were these two actions—i.e., the death of the animal and the ministry in the second apartment—somehow opposed to each other? Of course not. As two parts of the whole, both were crucial aspects of the same thing: the plan of salvation.

Now, if someone's understanding of what happened with the death of the animal was in tension or in contradiction with that person's understanding of the second-apartment ministry, then that person was misunderstanding either the death of the animal, the ministry in the second apartment, or both. These things, instituted by God, cannot be in opposition to each other. If opposition or contradiction arises, the problem is not in the rituals but in a person's understanding of those rituals.

In the same way, if a person's understanding of the Cross (symbolized by the death of the animal) is somehow in tension or in contradiction with their understanding of the pre-Advent judgment (symbolized by the second-apartment ministry), then that person misunderstands either the Cross, the judgment, or both. These things, instituted by God, cannot be in opposition. If opposition or contradiction arises, the problem is not in either the Cross or the judgment, but in a person's misunderstanding of these events.

And, finally, think about this: As Adventists, we believe that since 1844 we have been living in the anti-typical day of atonement. This means that the earthly Day of Atonement, which came once a year in the Jewish sanctuary ritual, was simply a model, a type, a small prophecy of this true Day of Atonement. In the same way that the animal sacrifices were types, symbols, of the Cross, the earthly Day of Atonement was a type, a symbol, of the real Day of Atonement, the one inaugurated in 1844 by Christ's work of judgment in the heavenly sanctuary.

If we are right, and we truly are living in the Day of Atonement, shouldn't that be good news? After all, what is atonement? Atonement is the work of God in saving us, right? How is atonement achieved? Only by Christ's blood, right? The law can't atone, right? Obedience can't atone, right? Good works can't atone, right? Atonement comes only one way, through what Christ has done for us, right? Of course.

Shouldn't, then, any "day" dedicated to atonement, that is, to God's work of saving us, be good news? Shouldn't we be rejoicing in the hope of living in the Day of Atonement rather than being distressed about it?

Of course.

How, then, have we Adventists turned the good news into bad news? That's another story. But, in reality, the problem isn't with the judgment, but with the false understanding of the judgment, as expressed by Brother Dale.

With these few points as background, let's take a look at the pre-Advent judgment in light of the Cross and see if Brother Dale's accusation that the teaching is anti-gospel is valid—or if it's of the same caliber as his "biblical evaluation" of the doctrine itself.

## JUDGMENT IN THE BIBLE

For the next few moments let's forget about 1844, "the investigative judgment," Ellen White, and Hiram Edson in the cornfield. Instead, read the following texts (I have purposely written them all out here because I want you to *read them*). Don't worry about whether these are "investigative judg-ment" texts or not; instead, focus on the following: Do these texts depict some sort of end-time judgment or judgments? When does this judgment, or judgments, occur? Who is judged? What criteria is used to judge? What role do works have in the judgment? How carefully are works and lives scrutinized? What are the results of the judgment? Let the texts speak for themselves independent of any preconceived judgment theology:

Not everyone that saith unto me, Lord, Lord, shall enter into the kingdom of heaven; but he that doeth the will of my Father which is in heaven. Many will say to me in that day, Lord, Lord, have we not prophesied in thy name? and in thy name have cast out devils? and in thy name done many wonderful works? And then will I profess unto them, I never knew you: depart from me, ye that work iniquity (Matthew 7:21-23).

Therefore is the kingdom of heaven likened unto a certain king, which would take account of his servants. And when he had begun to reckon, one was brought unto him, which owed him ten thou-sand talents. But forasmuch as he had not to pay, his lord com-manded him to be sold, and his wife, and children, and all that he had, and payment to be made. The servant therefore fell down, and worshipped him, saying, Lord, have patience with me, and I will pay thee all. Then the lord of that servant was moved with compas-sion, and loosed him, and forgave him the debt. But the same ser-vant went out, and found one of his fellowservants, which owed him an hundred pence: and he laid hands on him, and took him by the throat, saying, Pay me that thou owest. And his fellowservant fell down at his feet, and besought him, saying, Have patience with me, and I will pay thee all. And he would not: but went and cast him into prison, till he should pay the debt. So when his fellowservants saw what was done, they were very sorry, and came and told unto their lord all that was done. Then his lord, after that he had called him, said unto him, O thou wicked servant, I forgave thee all that debt, because thou desiredst me: Shouldst not thou also have had compassion on thy fellowservant, even as I had pity on thee? And his lord was wroth, and delivered him to the tormentors, till he should pay all that was due unto him. So likewise shall my heavenly Father do also unto you, if ye from your hearts forgive not every one his brother their trespasses (Matthew 18:23-35).

He that overcometh, the same shall be clothed in white raiment; and I will not blot his name out of the book of life, but I will confess his name before my Father, and before his angels (Revelation 3:5).

When the Son of man shall come in his glory, and all the holy angels with him, then shall he sit upon the throne of his glory: And before him shall be gathered all nations: and he shall separate them one from another, as a shepherd divideth his sheep from the goats: And he shall set the sheep on his right hand, but the goats on the left. Then shall the King say unto them on his right hand, Come, ye blessed of my Father, inherit the kingdom prepared for you from the foundation of the world: For I was an hungred, and ye gave me meat: I was thirsty, and ye gave me drink: I was a stranger, and ye took me in: Naked, and ye clothed me: I was sick, and ye visited me: I was in prison, and ye came unto me. Then shall the righteous answer him, saying, Lord, when saw we thee an hungred, and fed thee? or thirsty, and gave thee drink? When saw we thee a stranger, and took thee in? or naked, and clothed thee? Or when saw we thee sick, or in prison, and came unto thee? And the King shall answer and say unto them, Verily I say unto you, Inasmuch as ye have done it unto one of the least of these my brethren, ye have done it unto me. Then shall he also say unto them on the left hand, Depart from me, ye cursed, into everlasting fire, prepared for the devil and his angels: For I was an hungred, and ye gave me no meat: I was thirsty, and ye gave me no drink; I was a stranger, and ye took me not in: naked, and ye clothed me not: sick, and in prison, and ye visited me not. Then shall they also answer him, Lord, when saw we thee an hungred, or athirst, or a stranger, or naked, or sick, or in prison, and did not minister unto thee? Then shall he answer them, saying, Verily I say unto you, Inasmuch as ye did it not to one of the least of these, ye did it not to me. And these shall go away into everlasting punishment: but the righteous into life eternal (Matthew 25:31-46).

But why does thou judge thy brother? or why dost thou set at nought thy brother? for we shall all stand before the judgment seat of Christ. For it is written, As I live, saith the Lord, every knee shall bow to me, and every tongue shall confess to God. So then every one of us shall give account of himself to God (Romans 14:10-12).

And the ten horns out of this kingdom are ten kings that shall arise: and another shall rise after them; and he shall be diverse from the first, and he shall subdue three kings. And he shall speak great words against the most High, and shall wear out the saints of the most High, and think to change times and laws: and they shall be given into his hand until a time and times and the dividing of time. But the judgment shall sit, and they shall take away his dominion, to consume and to destroy it unto the end. And the kingdom and dominion, and the greatness of the kingdom under the whole heaven, shall be given to the people of the saints of the most High, whose kingdom is an everlasting kingdom, and all dominions shall serve and obey him (Daniel 7:24-27).

Let us hear the conclusion of the whole matter: Fear God, and keep his commandments: for this is the whole duty of man. For God shall bring every work into judgment, with every secret thing, whether it be good, or whether it be evil (Ecclesiastes 12:13, 14).

Every man's work shall be made manifest: for the day shall declare it, because it shall be revealed by fire; and the fire shall try every man's work of what sort it is (1 Corinthians 3:13).

For we must all appear before the judgment seat of Christ; that every one may receive the things done in his body, according to that he hath done, whether it be good or bad (2 Corinthians 5:10).

For we know him that hath said, Vengeance belongeth unto me, I will recompense, saith the Lord. And again, The Lord shall judge his people (Hebrews 10:30).

I am the true vine, and my Father is the husbandman. Every branch in me that beareth not fruit he taketh away: and every branch that beareth fruit, he purgeth it, that it may bring forth more fruit (John 15:1, 2).

For the Son of man shall come in the glory of his Father with his angels; and then he shall reward every man according to his works (Matthew 16:27).

And I saw the dead, small and great, stand before God; and the books were opened: and another book was opened, which is the book of life: and the dead were judged out of those things which were written in the books, according to their works (Revelation 20:12).

And, behold, I come quickly; and my reward is with me, to give every man according as his work shall be (Revelation 22:12).

For with what judgment ye judge, ye shall be judged (Matthew 7:2).

And if ye call on the Father, who without respect of persons judgeth according to every man's work, pass the time of your sojourning here in fear (1 Peter 1:17).

I said in mine heart, God shall judge the righteous and the wicked: for there is a time there for every purpose and for every work (Ecclesiastes 3:17).

For the time is come that judgment must begin at the house of God: and if it first begin at us, what shall the end be of them that obey not the gospel of God? (1 Peter 4:17).

But I say unto you, That every idle word that men shall speak, they shall give account thereof in the day of judgment. For by thy words thou shalt be justified, and by thy words thou shalt be condemned (Matthew 12:36, 37).

Then shall the kingdom of heaven be likened unto ten virgins, which took their lamps, and went forth to meet the bridegroom. And five of them were wise, and five were foolish. They that were foolish took their lamps, and took no oil with them: But the wise took oil in their vessels with their lamps. While the bridegroom tarried, they all slumbered and slept. And at midnight there was a cry made, Behold, the bridegroom cometh; go ye out to meet him. Then all those virgins arose, and trimmed their lamps. And the foolish said unto the wise, Give us of your oil; for our lamps are gone out. But the wise answered, saying, Not so; lest there be not enough for us and you: but go ye rather to them that sell, and buy for yourselves. And while they went to buy, the bridegroom came; and they that were ready went in with him to the marriage: and the door was shut. Afterward came also the other virgins, saying, Lord, Lord, open to us. But he answered and said, Verily I say unto you, I know you not (Matthew 25:1-12).

And at that time shall Michael stand up, the great prince which standeth for the children of thy people: and there shall be a time of trouble, such as never was since there was a nation even to that same time: and at that time thy people shall be delivered, every one that shall be found written in the book (Daniel 12:1).

Again, the kingdom of heaven is like unto a net, that was cast into the sea, and gathered of every kind: Which, when it was full, they drew to shore, and sat down, and gathered the good into vessels, but cast the bad away. So shall it be at the end of the world: the angels shall come forth, and sever the wicked from among the just, And shall cast them into the furnace of fire: there shall be wailing and gnashing of teeth (Matthew 13:47-50).

And Jesus answered and spake unto them again by parables, and said, The kingdom of heaven is like unto a certain king, which made a marriage for his son, And sent forth his servants to call them that were bidden to the wedding: and they would not come. Again, he sent forth other servants, saying, Tell them which are bidden, Behold, I have prepared my dinner: my oxen and my fatlings are killed, and all things are ready: come unto the marriage. But they made light of it, and went their ways, one to his farm, another to his merchandise: And the remnant took his servants, and entreated them spitefully, and slew them. But when the king heard thereof, he was wroth: and he sent forth his armies, and destroyed those murderers, and burned up their city. Then saith he to his servants, The wedding is ready, but they which were bidden were not worthy. Go ye therefore into the highways, and as many as ye shall find, bid to the marriage. So those servants went out into the highways, and gathered together all as many as they found, both bad and good: and the wedding was furnished with guests. And when the king came in to see the guests, he saw there a man which had not on a wedding garment: And he saith unto him, Friend, how camest thou in hither not having a wedding garment? And he was speechless. Then said the king to the servants, Bind him hand and foot, and take him away, and cast him into outer darkness; there shall be weeping and gnashing of teeth (Matthew 22:1-13).

But after thy hardness and impenitent heart treasurest up unto thyself wrath against the day of wrath and revelation of the righteous judgment of God (Romans 2:5).

And I saw another angel fly in the midst of heaven, having the everlasting gospel to preach unto them that dwell on the earth, and to every nation, and kindred, and tongue, and people, Saying with a loud voice, Fear God, and give glory to him; for the hour of his judgment is come: and worship him that made heaven, and earth, and the sea, and the fountains of waters (Revelation 14:6, 7).

Some men's sins are open beforehand, going before to judgment; and some men they follow after (1 Timothy 5:24).

A few points, apart from any distinctive Adventist theology, stand out from these verses:

First, there is some sort of final judgment (or judgments), a reckoning (or reckonings) near the end of time. This judgment (or judgments) is often directly associated with the Second Coming.

Second, among those judged are the professed followers of Christ. Both Jesus and Paul make it clear that those who profess to follow the Lord will be judged.

Third, a crucial element involved in this final reckoning is our works. This idea is a central focus of many of these texts.

Fourth, only two outcomes are presented—those who inherit the kingdom of God prepared "from the foundation of the world" or those who go into "everlasting punishment."

Fifth, some texts clearly show a judgment *prior* to the execution of the sentence—which makes sense. After all, even in human courts, who ever heard of a sentence being executed before judgment? In some texts, such as the parable of the wedding garment, this point is explicit—there's a judgment, an inspection of the guests' garments, and then condemnation. Revelation 22:12, in which the Lord says that when He returns, His reward is with Him, also implies a prior judgment. (Why would the reward already be with Him if there were not some means beforehand of determining who should get it?) Also 2 Corinthians 5:10 clearly teaches a reckoning prior to a final reward or punishment. This idea is found as well in Daniel 12:1, where those whose names are found in the book of life are delivered. Any kind of judgment according to works implies a reckoning of those works *before* the execution of the reward or punishment based on those works, be that judgment a hundred years or a hundred seconds before the punishment or vindication is carried out.

Also, it hardly seems unreasonable to see in Revelation 14:7, 8 a judgment *before* the Second Coming. The judgment is being proclaimed as part of the call to spread the gospel to the world; obviously, then, this judgment, presented as having already come, must take place prior to the Second Coming, because by then the gospel will have already been spread to the whole world (Matthew 24:14). In other words, the call to spread the gospel occurs at the same time as the message that judgment *has come*, which makes this judgment pre-Advent. Otherwise, why the call to proclaim the gospel to the world? The context of Revelation 14:4 through the end of the chapter, including the condemnation of Babylon (verse 8), the warning about worship of the beast (verses 10, 11), and the final harvest (verses 14-18), places this judgment before Christ returns.

And people can snort, snarl, and chortle all they want, but Daniel 7:24-27 teaches a heavenly judgment *before* God establishes His eternal kingdom, which doesn't happen until the Second Coming. Hence, a pre-Advent judgment.

## BROTHER DALE'S PRE-ADVENT JUDGMENT

In what must be the most hilarious line of his book, Brother Dale—in a section titled "The second coming of Christ reveals God's judgment"[8]—quotes Romans 2:5 (see above) and then writes: "The above text implies that the verdict has already been given. In that sense, it could be said to be a pre-Advent judgment."[9]

A pre-Advent *what? Judgment?* Kind of a strange admission, is it not, for a book dedicated to disproving the whole notion of a pre-Advent judgment?

Of course, Brother Dale then says that "this pre-advent judgment is not some investigative judgment where Jesus and the onlooking universe are pouring over the record books of heaven, measuring character to see who is worthy of eternal life."[10] That's fine; we'll come back to this later. But for now (and what's important for our discussion) Brother Ratzlaff admits to the existence of something which "could be said to be a pre-advent judgment." And though people may debate over its timing and nature, "a pre-advent judgment" would, by definition, include at least two points: It's a judgment, and it's pre-Advent—exactly what Adventists have been saying all along.

In fact, as Brother Dale continues to explain his "pre-advent judgment," he defines it exactly in the way most informed Adventists would define their concept of a pre-Advent judgment: "This judgment results from one's response to the gospel *when* it has been proclaimed, understood, and received or rejected. The last judgment simply reveals who by faith accepted God's free gift of eternal life and who did not."[11]

A loyal Seventh-day Adventist couldn't have described it better!

Brother Dale talks, first, about a person's "response" to the gospel. Though there are many kinds of responses (Luke 8:5-15), let's focus on those who profess to accept it, because here is where the debate about the investigative judgment rages—in the idea of a judgment for professed Christians.

Of course, those who accept Jesus as their Savior should manifest righteousness in their lives. That's basic Christianity:

But the fruit of the Spirit is love, joy, peace, longsuffering, gentleness, goodness, faith, meekness, temperance: against such there is no law. And they that are Christ's have crucified the flesh with the affections and lusts (Galatians 5:22-26).

Jesus said unto him, Thou shalt love the Lord thy God with all thy heart, and with all thy soul, and with all thy mind. This is the first and great commandment. And the second is like unto it, Thou shalt love thy neighbour as thyself (Matthew 22:37-39).

For this is the love of God, that we keep his commandments (1 John 5:3).

Jesus said that, in order to be saved, we "must be born again" (John 3:7), and a new birth implies "newness of life" (Romans 6:4). And what is new life if not manifested in our works, all of which are, as Brother Dale, says, "a response" to the gospel?

At the same time, many verses in the New Testament talk, not only about how someone who professes Christ must live, but also about the results of *not* obeying (Matthew 5:20; Revelation 22:15; James 1:26; Philippians 3:17-19; Galatians 6:7, 8; 1 Peter 4:17; 2 Thessalonians 1:8; Romans 6:16; Romans 2:5-11; 2 Peter 3:16; Ephesians 5:1-7, 19-21; Matthew 13:47-50).

Again, to quote Brother Dale: "The last judgment simply reveals who by faith accepted God's free gift of eternal life and who did not." A *last* what? Judgment. Last before what? The Second Coming, obviously. And in this last judgment before the Second Coming, what is it that reveals who has accepted God's gift by faith?

Works, what else?

> What doth it profit, my brethren, though a man say he hath faith, and have not works? can faith save him? If a brother or sister be naked, and destitute of daily food, And one of you say unto them, Depart in peace, be ye warmed and filled; notwithstanding ye give them not those things which are needful to the body; what doth it profit? Even so faith, if it hath not works, is dead, being alone. Yea, a man may say, Thou hast faith, and I have works: shew me thy faith without thy works, and I will shew thee my faith by my works. Thou believest that there is one God; thou doest well: the devils also believe, and tremble. But wilt thou know, O vain man, that faith without works is dead? (James 2:14-20).

For James, faith and works are inseparable. True faith can't exist without works any more than a square can exist without sides and edges. Anyone can claim faith, but only works reveal the claim's veracity. Works show whether faith is a living faith or a dead one (verse 20). James isn't teaching contrary to Pauline justification; he's merely showing that a faith which justifies must, of necessity, be a faith expressed in works.

Also, James's words about passing by someone naked and hungry fit with Christ's parable about "the least of these my brethren." Indeed, many of the judgment texts listed above tie in works directly with salvation and judgment, not because works save people in the judgment but because it's in the judgment that works reveal who has truly accepted Christ and His righteousness. Feeding the hungry, forgiving those who have sinned against us, speaking correct words, or doing good works—all these things simply reveal (as Brother Dale writes) "who by faith accepted God's free gift of eternal life and who did not." After all, who has fed enough hungry people, clothed enough naked people, said enough right words, or done enough good works to earn salvation? Paul's point in Romans is that we can't earn salvation, because then it's no longer grace (Romans 4:1-4).

What sinner can perform enough good deeds to bridge the gap between heaven and earth caused by sin? None, and James isn't saying that they can. James harmonizes with Paul when one understands that works—although they can't redeem us—are the expression, the manifestation, the existential reality of the redeemed. If we love God, we keep His commandments. We aren't justified by keeping those commandments, rather we keep them because we are already justified through Jesus.

*But how do I know if I have enough works to reveal a true faith?* That's a logical, but wrongly premised, question. It reflects that attitude of those who said, "Lord, Lord, have we not prophesied in thy name? and in thy name have cast out devils? and in thy name done many wonderful works?" (Matthew 7:22), or of the Pharisee, who said, "God, I thank thee, that I am not as other men are, extortioners, unjust, adulterers, or even as this publican. I fast twice in the week, I give tithes of all that I possess" (Luke 18:11, 12).

Instead, our attitude should be that of the publican, who smote his breast saying, "Lord, be merciful to me a sinner" (Luke 7:13). Anyone who has ever glimpsed the righteousness of Christ knows that he must throw himself on the mercy and grace of God, and that his works—whatever they are, however much done out of a pure and loving heart—are never enough. That is why we have to live by faith, trusting in God's promises that He will save us because of Jesus and Jesus alone. It's the realization of the inadequacy of our works that drives us to faith and to the promises of salvation through Christ. And it's that faith—the faith which believes God's promises—that transforms the life, a transformation revealed in works.

"We are accepted in the beloved," wrote Ellen White. "The sinner's defects are covered by the perfection and fullness of the Lord our righteousness."[12]

Now, logic alone might lead someone, after reading those words of Ellen White, to think, *Wow, now I can do whatever I want because I'm covered.* Instead, the response of a truly converted soul to these words would be, *Oh, Lord, thank You so much for this hope. Purge me, cleanse me, make me like You. I want to live worthy of the high calling I have in Jesus!*

Odd, isn't it, but the more one experiences the reality that his "defects are covered by the perfection and fullness of the Lord our righteousness," the more he will want to overcome those defects. The more one understands that he's saved by Christ's obedience to the law (as opposed to his own), the more he will want to obey that law. However much logic alone might suggest the opposite response *(I'm covered, so let's party!)*, those who have experienced Christ's covering their sins want more than ever to have those sins purged from their lives. They want a faith expressed by works—works which (again, to quote Brother Dale's pre-advent judgment) reveal whether they "by faith accepted God's free gift of eternal life."

## THE GOOD NEWS OF THE JUDGMENT

Earlier, Brother Dale mocked the idea of Jesus and the onlooking universe going over the books in a pre-Advent judgment. Yet the image of books, or a book, is used by the Bible writers in connection with the question of salvation and condemnation.[13] Many of the verses listed above unambiguously show that judgment involves some sort of scrutiny of the attitudes and works of those judged; after all, what is a judgment without such a scrutiny? Also, didn't Jesus say that we shall give an account of "every idle word," (Matthew 12:36)? *Every* idle word? Is this not the same Jesus who said that "the hairs on your head are numbered" (Matthew 10:30), who knows when a sparrow falls to the ground (Matthew 10:29), who said that He shall bring "every work into judgment, with every secret thing" (Ecclesiastes 12:14)? *Every* work? *Every* secret thing? Thus, the whole idea of books, and a scrutiny of works, in the judgment shouldn't be so cavalierly dismissed.

Yet (and this gets to the crux of the matter) how could any sinner stand when *every* idle word, *every* secret thing, comes into judgment? I'm a goner for what I've done in public, much less in secret! Who among earth's sinful billions could stand justified before God in judgment when every idle word and every secret thing is exposed?

None. But the good news of the judgment is that Jesus, in His righteousness, gets us through the judgment because He stands there in our place. Otherwise all of us would be lost because none of us, no matter how good our works, have enough righteousness to stand before a Holy God. Unless we are clothed in a perfect righteousness that none of us ourselves possess or could ever earn (no matter how sincerely and in faith we have tried), we would have to stand in our own works, our own righteousness—and who wants to do that before the all-seeing eyes of a God who knows our deepest thoughts and innermost secrets, thoughts and secrets that we would be horrified to tell our most intimate confidant?

Yet the good news of the judgment is that we don't have to stand in our own righteousness. We can stand in the righteousness of Jesus. Just because we are judged by works doesn't mean that we are saved by them. We are saved, instead, only through the righteousness of Jesus, which is credited to us by faith. This righteousness covers us the moment we surrender ourselves completely to Christ and claim His righteousness for ourselves—and it stays with us (though not un-conditionally) right through the judgment. "There is therefore now no condemnation to them which are in Christ Jesus, who walk not after the flesh but after the Spirit" (Romans 8:1). No condemnation— not now, and certainly not in the judgment. After all, what good would being covered by that righteousness do any of us if we don't have it when we need it the most—in the judgment?

Anyone who makes it through the pre-Advent judgment will do so only because that person has Jesus standing in his stead. What else would get them through? Their works? Their obedience to the law? The number of times they fed the hungry? Please!

> Who is he that condemneth? It is Christ that died, yea rather, that is risen again, who is even at the right hand of God, who also maketh intercession for us (Romans 8:34).

> Wherefore he is able also to save them to the uttermost that come unto God by him, seeing he ever liveth to make intercession for them (Hebrews 7:25).

> For Christ is not entered into the holy places made with hands, which are the figures of the true; but into heaven itself, now to appear in the presence of God for us (Hebrews 9:24).

> Whither the forerunner is for us entered, even Jesus, made an high priest for ever after the order of Melchisedec (Hebrews 6:20).

Does this intercession for us suddenly end on the Day of Atonement, the day of judgment, when we need it most? Or is that intercession for us the only thing that gets us through the Day of Atonement?

Again, how does atonement occur? Through works? Through the law? Through feeding the hungry? Clothing the naked? Through speaking right words? Through bearing fruit? Through visiting inmates? Through developing a Christlike character? No, because if good works would have done it, Christ wouldn't have had to die for us. Atonement comes only through the blood of Jesus, regardless of the role of works in judgment.

Most Adventists, when taught the pre-Advent judgment, have been taken into the Most Holy Place without blood, which leads only to death because in the Most Holy Place is the law, and the law condemns, not pardons. Yet atonement is about pardon, not condemnation. The law has no power to save, no power to atone, no power to pardon, no power to enable people to obey any more than staring into a mirror can make an ugly face pretty. That's why Paul wrote that all those who "rely on the works of the law are under a curse" (Galatians 3:10, RSV). Paul didn't write that those who *obeyed* the law were under a curse, for that's contrary to many of God's clear commands about obedience to the law (Revelation 14:12; 22:14; 1 John 5:2, 3; James 2:10). Instead he says that those who *rely* on these works for salvation are under a curse because those works cannot save them.

In the Levitical system, the high priest never went into the Most Holy Place (symbolic of the judgment) without blood, because it was the Day of *Atonement*, and only blood atones for sin (read Leviticus 16). The key element, stressed over and over, is blood, not law, because blood, not law, atones.

And he shall take of the *blood* of the bullock, and sprinkle it with his finger upon the mercy seat eastward; and before the mercy seat shall he sprinkle of the *blood* with his finger seven times. Then shall he kill the goat of the sin offering, that is for the people, and bring his *blood* within the vail, and do with that *blood* as he did with the *blood* of the bullock, and sprinkle it upon the mercy seat, and before the mercy seat. . . . And he shall go out unto the altar that is before the Lord, and make an atonement for it; and shall take of the *blood* of the bullock, and of the *blood* of the goat, and put it upon the horns of the altar round about. And he shall sprinkle of the *blood* upon it with his finger seven times, and cleanse it, and hallow it from the uncleanness of the children of Israel (Leviticus 16:14, 15, 18, 19, italics supplied).

Every drop of that blood symbolized the blood of Christ, the only blood that truly makes atonement: "Forasmuch as ye know that ye were not redeemed with corruptible things, as silver and gold, from your vain conversation received by tradition from your fathers; But with the precious blood of Christ, as of a lamb without blemish and without spot" (1 Peter 1:18, 19). And though people are judged by works, it's blood, not works, that gets the repentant sinner through the judgment.

Perhaps the clearest example of Christ's righteousness covering us in the judgment comes from one of Jesus' judgment parables, the story of the wedding feast. After those who were first called rejected the invitation, the "servants went out into the highways, and gathered together all as many as they found, both bad and good: and the wedding was furnished with guests. And when the king came in to see the guests, he saw there a man which had not on a wedding garment: And he saith unto him, Friend, how camest thou in hither not having a wedding garment? And he was speechless. Then said the king to the servants, Bind him hand and foot, and take him away, and cast him into outer darkness; there shall be weeping and gnashing of teeth" (Matthew 22:10-13).

What determined whether the man stayed or left? The garment that the owner gave to the guests (a custom in that time and place). The person responded to the invitation, but he never took what was offered him. What is that garment, other than the righteousness of Christ? "I will greatly rejoice in the Lord, my soul shall be joyful in my God; for he hath clothed me with the garments of salvation, he hath covered me with the robe of righteousness, as a bridegroom decketh himself with ornaments, and as a bride adorneth herself with her jewels" (Isaiah 61:10). The guest, heeding the invitation, but not the conditions, refused what the owner offered him.

Notice, the parable said that both the good and the bad came. It didn't say whether the man without the garment was good or bad. In one sense it made no difference. In the judgment, before God, we all—"good" or "bad"—stand condemned without a garment. What the guest needed at the wedding is the same thing that we need in the judgment, something covering us. Otherwise, we will be cast out where there is weeping and gnashing of teeth. That covering, symbolized by the garment in the parable, is the righteousness of Jesus, credited to His followers by faith, and it is their only hope in the judgment.

Another powerful presentation from Scripture about judgment comes from the Old Testament:

And he shewed me Joshua the high priest standing before the angel of the Lord, and Satan standing at his right hand to resist him. And the Lord said unto Satan, The Lord rebuke thee, O Satan; even the Lord that hath chosen Jerusalem rebuke thee: is not this a brand plucked out of the fire? Now Joshua was clothed with filthy garments, and stood before the angel. And he answered and spake unto those that stood before him, saying, Take away the filthy garments from him. And unto him he said, Behold, I have caused thine iniquity to pass from thee, and I will clothe thee with change of raiment. And I said, Let them set a fair mitre upon his head. So they set a fair mitre upon his head, and clothed him with garments. And the angel of the Lord stood by (Zechariah 3:1-5).

At first, Joshua is clothed in what? Filthy garments (the word translated "filthy" comes from a Hebrew word for human excrement, see Deuteronomy 23:13; Ezekiel 4:12; Isaiah 28:8), a graphic portrayal of the high priest's clothes. What does that stained garment represent, other than the sins and iniquities of God's people? Remember, this is the high priest here and, as such, he is representative of the corporate body; thus God's people, His chosen ones, His church, are depicted as in a terrible spiritual state. The high priest as a representative of the whole people becomes especially apparent on (interestingly enough) the Day of Atonement, a time of corporate repentance and atonement.

Zechariah's vision evokes many parallels to the first two chapters of Job in which Satan appears before the Lord in some heavenly assize where he makes charges and accusations against someone serving the Lord. The Hebrew word translated "to resist him" (Zechariah 3:1) actually comes from the same root word as the name Satan itself (stn), and it means to "to be or to act as an adversary," or "to accuse."

As in Job, this interaction between the Angel of the Lord (who is Christ) and Satan doesn't occur in a vacuum. Christ spoke to those who "stood before him" (Zechariah 3:4), just as in Job the contention between God and Satan occurred in the presence of the "sons of God" (Job 1:6). See also the heavenly judgment scene of Daniel 7:10, where other beings are present.

Notice, too, what happens in Zechariah's vision. Though Satan attacks Joshua, making accusations against him, who is rebuked? Joshua, standing there in the shame of his excrement-covered garments (a symbol of a sinful people), or Satan?

"The Lord rebuke thee, O Satan, even the Lord that has chosen Jerusalem rebuke thee." Obviously, Christ is there to defend His people, not to accuse them. Talk about an Old Testament expression of the gospel!

The Lord then says that Joshua is a brand plucked out of the fire (the children of Israel, after years of captivity, would have been destroyed were it not for the Lord bringing them back to the land). Now, what brand ever plucked itself out of the fire? None. It has to be plucked out by something other than itself. In the same way, none of us can be saved by anything other than God. Here, too, we see another example of a gospel principle: God doing for us what we could never do for ourselves.

But the most important part comes when the order is given to remove the filthy garments and to have new ones placed on Joshua. Notice, Jesus doesn't tell Joshua to cleanse his own garments or to take off the garments and put on new ones. Instead, the Lord has it done Himself; He has Joshua's garments changed.

"Behold, I have caused thine iniquity to pass from thee, and I will clothe thee with change of raiment." It's God who gets rid of the old garments and puts on the new ones; it's the Lord who causes Joshua's iniquity to pass from him and who clothes him in righteousness. Again, what could be a better depiction of the plan of salvation?

Now, after the Lord works this change of garments, He says to Joshua, "If thou wilt walk in my ways, and if thou wilt keep my charge, then thou shalt also judge my house, and shalt also keep my courts, and I will give thee places to walk among these that stand by" (Zechariah 3:7). In other words, *after* He rebukes Satan, *after* He removes the dirty garments, *after* He covers Joshua in clean garments, He *then* gives Joshua the clear command to walk in His ways and to keep His charges. God didn't say, "Joshua, do these things, keep My ways and My charges, and then I will remove your dirty garments and give you new ones." Instead, it was *after* He saved Joshua, after He removed the guilt and stains of sin, and covered him in His own righteousness that He gave Joshua the command about faithfulness and obedience. Thus, Joshua's obedience wasn't the *cause* of his change of garments; it was the *result* of having them already changed. If this isn't a depiction of how we are saved, what is?

Ellen White, in a vision about this chapter, interprets it in a gospel-orientated manner as well. How ironic that Brother Dale should harp against Ellen White and her writings about the investigative judgment because they (as he claims) contradict the gospel. Yet if he had read her carefully, particularly this section and others like it, he would have never hammered out such error.

After describing the background to Zechariah 3, Ellen White writes:

The high priest cannot defend himself or his people from Satan's accusations. He does not claim that Israel are free from fault. In his filthy garments, symbolizing the sins of the people, which he bears as their representative, he stands before the Angel, confessing their guilt, yet pointing to their repentance and humiliation, relying upon the mercy of a sin-pardoning Redeemer and in faith claiming the promises of God.[14]

As the intercession of Joshua is accepted, the command is given, "Take away the filthy garments from him," and to Joshua the Angel declares, " 'Behold, I have caused thine iniquity to pass from thee, and I will clothe thee with change of raiment.' So they set a fair miter upon his head, and clothed him with garments." His own sins and those of his people were pardoned. Israel were clothed with "change of raiment"—the righteousness of Christ imputed to them.[15]

For Ellen White, the taking away of the sin-stained garments is equated with the pardoning of sins. They are forgiven, covered by the blood of Christ.

She also talks about how Satan accuses God's people in all ages, and how the devil "exults in their defective characters."[16] By countless devices, the most subtle and the most cruel, Satan

endeavors to secure their condemnation. Man cannot meet these charges himself. In his sin-stained garments, confessing his guilt, he stands before God. But Jesus our Advocate presents an effectual plea in behalf of all who by repentance and faith have committed the keeping of their souls to Him. *He pleads their cause and vanquishes their accuser by the mighty arguments of Calvary.* His perfect obedience to God's law, even unto the death of the cross, has given Him all power in heaven and in earth, and He claims of His Father mercy and reconciliation for guilty man. To the accuser of His people He declares: " 'The Lord rebuke thee, O Satan.' These are the purchase of My blood, brands plucked from the burning." Those who rely upon Him in faith receive the comforting assurance: "Behold, I have caused thine iniquity to pass from thee, and I will clothe thee with change of raiment." All that have put on the robe of Christ's righteousness will stand before Him as chosen and faithful and true. Satan has no power to pluck them out of the hand of Christ.[17] (Italics supplied.)

Anti-gospel? For some reason, these quotes from Ellen White never made it into Brother Dale's book. Talking about these same struggling saints, she continues:

> Their only hope is in the mercy of God; their only defense will be prayer. As Joshua was pleading before the Angel, so the remnant church, with brokenness of heart and earnest faith, will plead for pardon and deliverance through Jesus their Advocate. They are fully conscious of the sinfulness of their lives, they see their weakness and unworthiness, and as they look upon themselves they are ready to despair. The tempter stands by to accuse them, as he stood by to resist Joshua. He points to their filthy garments, their defective characters. He presents their weakness and folly, their sins of ingratitude, their unlikeness to Christ, which has dishonored their Redeemer. He endeavors to affright the soul with the thought that their case is hopeless, that the stain of their defilement will never be washed away. He hopes to so destroy their faith that they will yield to his temptations, turn from their allegiance to God, and receive the mark of the beast.[18]

Who focuses on their sins, their filthy garments, their weakness and their folly, their ingratitude and unlikeness to Christ? The Lord or Satan? It's Satan, not the Lord, because Christ already knows their faults, their defects, their sins. Christ, however, is there to plead their case for them anyway, because this is the Day of Atonement, and atonement is about acquittal, not condemnation.

Notice the timing. Satan tries to discourage them so that they will receive "the mark of the beast." This, then, refers to the final generation, those living at the end of time when the judgment ends, probation closes, and Christ returns.

> The fact that the acknowledged people of God are represented as standing before the Lord in filthy garments should lead to humility and deep searching of heart on the part of all who profess His name. Those who are indeed purifying their souls by obeying the truth will have a most humble opinion of themselves. The more closely they view the spotless character of Christ, the stronger will

be their desire to be conformed to His image, and the less will they see of purity or holiness in themselves. *But while we should realize our sinful condition, we are to rely upon Christ as our righteousness, our sanctification, and our redemption. We cannot answer the charges of Satan against us. Christ alone can make an effectual plea in our behalf. He is able to silence the accuser with arguments founded not upon our merits, but on His own.*[19] (Italics supplied.)

What answers the devil's accusations? Only one thing: the merits of Jesus, that righteousness which He wrought out in His life and which He freely offers to all who will claim it in faith, both for now and in the judgment. Those few lines italicized above are a powerful expression of the gospel and judgment; they show how an understanding of the second apartment ministry helps elaborate and explain the Cross; they show how there is no tension or contradiction between the Cross and judgment; and finally, they show that the judgment is good news because our great hope in the judgment is the merits of Christ.

"Zechariah's vision of Joshua and the Angel," Ellen White writes, "applies with peculiar force to the experience of God's people in the closing up of the great day of atonement."[20] In other words, Satan accuses God's people—those who have "defective characters," who have "weakness and folly," who have been "very faulty," and who are aware of the "sinfulness of their lives"—while they are defended by Jesus, who pleads the arguments of the Cross in their behalf because nothing else will get them through the judgment. They need the change of raiment, "the righteousness of Christ," she says, "imputed to them."

Here is Ellen White again, on the same topic:

While Jesus is pleading for the subjects of His grace, Satan accuses them before God as transgressors. The great deceiver has sought to lead them into skepticism, to cause them to lose confidence in God, to separate themselves from his love, and to break his law. Now he points to the record of their lives, to the defects of character, the unlikeness to Christ, which has dishonored their Redeemer, to all the sins that he has tempted them to commit, and because of these he claims them as his subjects.

Jesus does not excuse their sins, but shows their penitence and faith, and, claiming for them forgiveness, He lifts His wounded hands before the Father and the holy angels, saying, "I know them by name. I have graven them on the palms of my hands. 'The sacrifices of God are a broken spirit; a broken and a contrite heart, O God, thou wilt not despise' " (Psalm 51:17). And to the accuser of His people He declares, "The Lord rebuke thee, O Satan; even the Lord that hath chosen Jerusalem rebuke thee: Is not this a brand plucked out of the fire?" Zechariah 3:2. Christ will clothe His faithful ones with His own righteousness, that He may present them to His Father "a glorious church, not having spot, or wrinkle, or any such thing" Ephesians 5:27. Their names stand enrolled in the book of life, and concerning them it is written, "They shall walk with Me in white: for they are worthy." Revelation 3:4.[21]

Yet Brother Dale insists that investigative judgment, as taught by Ellen White, is anti-gospel. She says further regarding Zechariah's vision:

> The people of God have been in many respects very faulty. Satan has an accurate knowledge of the sins which he has tempted them to commit, and he presents these in the most exaggerated light, declaring: "Will God banish me and my angels from His presence, and yet reward those who have been guilty of the same sins? Thou canst not do this, O Lord, in justice. Thy throne will not stand in righteousness and judgment. Justice demands that sentence be pronounced against them."
>
> But while the followers of Christ have sinned, they have not given themselves to the control of evil. They have put away their sins, and have sought the Lord in humility and contrition, and the divine Advocate pleads in their behalf. He who has been most abused by their ingratitude, who knows their sin, and also their repentance, declares: " 'The Lord rebuke thee, O Satan.' I gave My life for these souls. They are graven upon the palms of My hands."[22]

Is that too much to ask of the followers of Christ, who claim Him as Lord, that they not give themselves over to *the control of evil?* Not giving themselves over to the control of evil is much different, is it not, than being a faithful Christian who loves the Lord but who struggles—not always successfully—with self, with sin, and with temptations?

Of course it is, and yet Ellen White doesn't express the idea half as strongly as does John: "Little children, let no man deceive you: he that doeth righteousness is righteous, even as he [Jesus] is righteous. He that committeth sin is of the devil; for the devil sinneth from the beginning" (1 John 3:6). Or as Paul: "Now the works of the flesh are manifest, which are these; adultery,

fornication, uncleanness, lasciviousness, idolatry, witchcraft, hatred, vari-
ance, emulations, wrath, strife, seditions, heresies, envyings, murders, drunk-
enness, revellings, and such like: of the which I tell you before, as I have also
told you in time past, that they which do such things shall not inherit the
kingdom of God" (Galatians 5:19-21). Or, especially, as does Jesus: "But I
say unto you, That whosoever looketh on a woman to lust after her hath
committed adultery with her already in his heart. And if thy right eye offend
thee, pluck it out, and cast it from thee: for it is profitable for thee that one
of thy members should perish, and not that thy whole body should be cast
into hell. And if thy right hand offend thee, cut it off, and cast it from thee:
for it is profitable for thee that one of thy members should perish, and not
that thy whole body should be cast into hell" (Matthew 5:28-30).

We can talk grace, blood, forgiveness, justification, and substitution all
we want, but those who use these concepts as a cover for iniquity are
precisely the ones, the only ones, who need to fear the judgment (Matthew 7:22, 23). In contrast, those depicted by Ellen White in her interpretation of the vision in Zechariah concerning the judgment, far from negating the gospel, bring it to a glorious climax in their own lives. The
judgment isn't a time when God decides to accept or reject us; it's simply
the time when God finalizes *our choice* and recognizes whether or not we
have accepted Him, a choice inevitably made manifest by our works.

## THE SUM OF THE MATTER

As we have seen, no contradiction exists between the death of the
animal (symbolic of the Cross) on the Day of Atonement and the ministry
of the high priest in the Most Holy Place (symbolic of the judgment). How
could there be? Both are two parts of the same process, God's plan of
salvation for the lost race.

We have seen, too, that the crucial element on the Day of Atonement
was blood, not the law, because only blood atones for sin.

Finally, atonement is God's work in our behalf, something that He does
for us because we could never do it for ourselves.

Keeping these few points in mind, how do we understand the pre-
Advent judgment in light of the blood of the Cross?

First, we recognize that we all are sinners, that all of us have fallen short
of God's perfect law, and that we all, left on our own, stand condemned
before God (Romans 3:10, 23; 5:12; Galatians 3:22).

Second we recognize that the Lord has provided a way out through
Jesus. Christ paid the penalty for every sinner. By doing that He reconciled

heaven to earth. No more was there an automatic condemnation of the human race. Ideally, every human being could have been saved (Romans 5:15-21; 2 Corinthians 5:19; Hebrews 2:9).

Third, because we are sinners, we have no possibility of standing before a Holy God in the judgment. The good news of the gospel is that Jesus, by His death, offers us the perfect merits of His life. This righteousness comes to us only by faith, not by works, because if it were by works, we could earn it (Romans 4:3-6; 3:28; 4:13-16; Galatians 2:16; 3:11).

Fourth, our faith is made manifest in our lives by our works, which—though unable to pay the debt owed to the law—reveal that we have been saved by Jesus Christ, who has given us a new life. Works are an inseparable aspect of our Christian life, the undeniable fruit of a life hidden with Christ in God. They are the expression of a soul that has been born again, the requisite response of a person who loves God because of the Cross. To separate works from biblical faith is like separating roundness from a circle; whatever you have in the end, it's not biblical faith (John 3:3; 14:15; Romans 6:4; Colossians 3:3; 10; 1 Thessalonians 4:3; Titus 3:5; Matthew 7:24-27; Ephesians 5:9; 1 John 5:2).

Fifth, there is a judgment of believers, of those who have professed faith in Christ (Romans 14:10-12; Matthew 22:1-13; Revelation 22:12; 1 Peter 1:17). This judgment merely reveals whether we have truly accepted Christ or not, a choice that is made manifest by our works. In Brother Dale's own words, "We see, then, that men are *judged* by their response to the good news of the gospel. The light of the mercy of God has been brightly revealed in Christ. Now, the darkness of sin has no excuse"[23] (italics supplied). Again, although works don't save us in the judgment, they reveal "who by faith accepted God's free gift of eternal life and who did not."[24]

How does this happen? A professed follower's life comes up before God: every work, every secret thing, every idle word, comes into review (Matthew 12:36; Ecclesiastes 12:14; 3:17; 2 Corinthians 5:10; Romans 14:10-12; Psalm 135:14; Hebrews 10:30). Before such a scrutiny who could stand? No one (Romans 3:23; 3:10; Galatians 3:22; 1 Timothy 1:15). However, for the true followers of Christ, Jesus stands as their Advocate, their Representative, their Intercessor in heaven (Romans 8:34: Hebrews 7:25; 9:24; 6:20; 1 John 2:1;). And though they have nothing in and of themselves to give them merit before God, though they have no works that are good enough to justify them before the Lord, their lives—however faulty, however defective—nevertheless reveal their true repentance and faith (James 2:14-20; 1 John 5:3; 4:20; John 14:15; Matthew 7:24-27). How they treated the poor, the needy, those in prison, how they forgave as they were forgiven, the words they spoke, the deeds they did (Matthew 18:23-35; 25:31-46; 12:36, 37; 7:2)—while these things could never justify them before God, while they could never answer the demands of a broken law, these acts reveal those who have accepted Christ as their Substitute and His righteousness alone, which covers them like a garment and gets them through the judgment (1 John 2:1; Matthew 22:1-14; Zechariah 3:1-5; Leviticus 16; Romans 8:34; 8:1; Hebrews 9:24;).

Again, the question shouldn't be, *How do I know that I will have enough works to show that I have faith?* Going on the assumption that we will never have enough good works, we must lean only on the merits of Jesus, who died for our sins and whose perfect life is credited to us by faith. This is our only hope of salvation, now and in the judgment. Or, as Ellen White so clearly expressed it:

> But while we should realize our sinful condition, we are to rely upon Christ as our righteousness, our sanctification, and our redemption. We cannot answer the charges of Satan against us. Christ alone can make an effectual plea in our behalf. He is able to silence the accuser with arguments founded not upon our merits, but on His own.[25]

The futility of our works for salvation should cause us to lean totally on the mercy and merits of Christ. Then, out of love and thankfulness for the assurance of salvation that is ours through Christ, we serve Him with all our heart, soul, mind, and body—a service that's expressed in works. How else could it be?

The judgment, then, is the climactic application of the gospel in our lives. It's Leviticus 16, the Day of Atonement, consummated in our behalf. The judgment, apart from the gospel, is like Leviticus 16 without blood: all you come up with is death.

The claim that the investigative judgment is anti-gospel reveals nothing about the investigative judgment, but it reveals much about those who make the claim. Brother Dale is a victim of a folk version of the judgment that is based solely on a *misuse* of Ellen White, on a few select quotes taken out of the context of her whole writing, and upon which a complete edifice of a perfectionistic, anti-gospel theology has been built, a theology that's not only contrary to the Bible but to Ellen White. How tragic, and ironic, especially in light of Ellen White's explanation of the vision of "Joshua and the Angel," a gospel-centered depiction of the pre-

Advent judgment that puts Christ's death for us at the center of the judgment, the only way it can be understood.

Brother Dale, however sincerely, spends four hundred pages fighting a folk version of Adventist theology—not the true one, the one that more and more Adventists are understanding, the one that, indeed, Ellen White herself taught.

---

[1] Ratzlaff, Dale, *The Cultic Doctrine of Seventh-day Adventists* (Life Assurance Ministries, Glendale, AZ) 1998, unnumbered page [2].

[2] *Ibid.,* unnumbered page [9].

[3] Ibid., p. 236.

[4] *Ibid.*

[5] *Ibid.,* p. 238.

[6] *Ibid.,* p. 353.

[7] *Ibid.,* p. 236.

[8] *Ibid.,* p. 260.

[9] *Ibid.*

[10] *Ibid.*

[11] *Ibid,* pp.260, 261.

[12] Ellen White, *Our High Calling,* p. 51.

[13] "And at that time shall Michael stand up, the great prince which standeth for the children of thy people: and there shall be a time of trouble, such as never was since there was a nation even to that same time: and at that time thy people shall be delivered, every one that shall be found written in the book" (Daniel 12:1). "The judgment was set, and the books were opened" (Daniel 7:10). "And I saw the dead, small and great, stand before God; and the books were opened: and another book was opened, which is the book of life: and the dead were judged out of those things which were written in the books, according to their works" (Revelation 20:12). "And whosoever was not found written in the book of life was cast into the lake of fire" (Revelation 20:15). "Let them be blotted out of the book of the living, and not be written with the righteous" (Psalm 69:28). "Yet now, if thou wilt forgive their sin—; and if not, blot me, I pray thee, out of thy book which thou hast written. And the Lord said unto Moses, Whosoever hath sinned against me, him will I blot out of my book" (Exodus 32:32, 33). "And they shall bring the glory and honour of the nations into it. And there shall in no wise enter into it any thing that defileth, neither whatsoever worketh abomination, or maketh a lie: but they which are written in the Lamb's book of life" (Revelation 21:26, 27). "He that overcometh, the same shall be clothed in white raiment; and I will not blot out his name out of the book of life, but I will confess his name before my Father, and before his angels" (Revelation 3:5).

[14] Ellen White, *Testimonies for the Church,* vol. 5, pp. 468, 469.

[15] *Ibid.,* p. 469.

[16] *Ibid.,* p. 470.

[17] *Ibid.,* p.471.

[18] *Ibid.,* p. 473.

[19] Ibid., pp. 471, 472.

[20] *Ibid.,* p. 472.

[21] Ellen White, *The Great Controversy,* p. 484.

[22] Ellen White, *Testimonies for the Church,* vol. 5, p. 474.

[23] CDSDA, p. 260.

[24] *Ibid.,* pp.260, 261.

[25] Ellen White, *Testimonies for the Church,* vol.5, p. 472.

# CHAPTER SEVEN

# THE
# GIFT
## OF
# PROPHECY

German philosopher Immanuel Kant once constructed an entire philosophy based on the difference between two types of sentences. The first type (called analytic) is a statement such as: "The circle is round." By definition, a circle is round, so the predicate of the sentence, "is round," adds nothing to the subject, "the circle."

The second type (called synthetic) is a statement such as: "The circle is red." Circles, to be circles, have to be round; they don't have to be red. So the predicate, "is red," does add something to the subject that we wouldn't get from its definition alone.

Now when we make the statement, "Ellen White is a prophet," what qualities and attributes do we automatically assume come packaged with the word "prophet"? "Inerrancy"? "Character perfection"? "Immutability"? "Originality"? Do these attributes belong to "prophet" as "round" does to "circle"? Or are they notions that don't of necessity, or by definition, belong there?

These questions are important because Adventists believe that Ellen White's role was that of a prophet of God. And as such, she is often the catalyst, the major issue, that has started many on the painful path out the door of the Seventh-day Adventist Church. Brother Dale is no exception. In *The Cultic Doctrine of Seventh-Day Adventists* he makes Ellen White *the* major issue, even though she shouldn't be. That she is—not just with Brother Dale, but with so many others—says a lot about how we have mishandled this wonderful God-given gift.

For me, the question of Ellen White's prophetic calling isn't a question. For me, it's settled—like the existence of God, or of Jesus being the Messiah, or of the continued validity of the seventh-day Sabbath. I've been there, done that. Though questions, tensions, and issues may remain in these areas, the basic points themselves have been resolved in my mind long ago.

What's still not fully resolved for me—what's still fermenting, still brewing, in my brain is this: *What should be the role and authority of Ellen G. White in the church today?* Again, you might as well try to convince me that Sun Myung Moon is, as Moonies claim, the one sent by God to finish Christ's work as try to convince me that Ellen White didn't manifest the "spirit of prophecy." What isn't a given, however, is just what her role in the church should be.

Yet I'm not overly concerned about totally understanding that role because I know what I need to know to be a Seventh-day Adventist from *my Bible alone.* Take Ellen White away from me, and the key teachings that have made me an Adventist—a six-day Creation of life on earth, the death and resurrection of Jesus, a literal Second Coming from heaven, the Sabbath, the state of the dead, the sanctuary and 1844—all remain, with or without her.

That my life has been incomparably blessed by her, that her writings have greatly strengthened my faith, that her witness and ministry are a great source of continued encouragement to me, that she has helped clarify in my mind many important issues, that she inspires me as no other noncanonical author ever has, that I believe she was a messenger from God—to all these I answer an unequivocal and unapologetic "Yes!" But she has not been, nor through the grace of God will she ever be, the foundation of my faith. As Adventists, when we wave the Reformation banner of *sola scriptura,* we ought to mean it.

## PERSONAL TESTIMONY

I didn't reach this position regarding Ellen White's ministry by accident. I got here instead by a long and sometimes torturous road. I believe, too, that I've managed (through the grace of God) to stay on the right path, however far from the perfect center I am and probably always will be.

In my earliest days as a new Adventist, I held what I now deem an erroneous and potentially dangerous view of Ellen White's ministry and inspiration, a view prevalent in the church and one that has caused many, such as Dale Ratzlaff, to leave.

My first encounter with Ellen White goes back before I was an Adventist. Having just had some powerful supernatural experiences, I stepped through the door of the occult, thinking that here were answers to my questions about the meaning of life. On my way to the university library to start reading about the occult, I stopped at a health food store. When I mentioned to the owner where I was going (to the library), and why (to read about the occult), he tried to warn me about the devil (which at that point in my life was like warning me that Santa wouldn't come down the chimney on Christmas Eve if I were bad). Laughing him off as I left, I nevertheless did take a book that he gave me.

I then went to the library, pulled a book on the occult off the shelf, and started reading it. After reading the first chapter of the occult book, I put it back on the shelf (though not where it belonged, because I wasn't enrolled in school at that time and couldn't check out books. So I hid it to keep anyone else from checking it out before I came back and finished reading it.).

Anyway, the bottom line is this: On that hot summer Florida afternoon in the University of Florida library, I had in one hand, for the first time in my life, a book on the occult, while in my other hand, literally, for the first time in my life, was the book the owner of the health food store had given me. Can you guess what the title of that book might be?

Of course. *The Great Controversy*.

At that time, no inkling about what was happening flowed through my mind. Though a few days afterward Christ came and converted me (ending my foray into the occult), it was much later that I realized the significance of having an occult book in one hand and *The Great Controversy* in the other—both for the first time ever!

Thus, from the beginning, Ellen White has played a role in my Christian walk. Nevertheless, when first presented with her, and her claims, I was resistant, and understandably so (after all, the prophetic gift is heavy). At one point after my conversion, yet a few months before joining the Adventist Church, I read something that she wrote about a verse in Timothy which she had attributed to Paul. Still hardly literate biblically, I thought that Timothy, not Paul, had written the New Testament book of Timothy. I was thrilled! I had found an error in Ellen White! She couldn't, then, be a prophet. And therefore I didn't have to accept her and the things she said that stomped on my toes.

Not long after, I discovered my error about the authorship of Timothy, which defused my great reason for rejecting Ellen White. Yet the incident is instructive, for though I soon believed in her gift, I went into that belief assuming infallibility as a given attribute of a genuine prophet (after all, could a prophet from a perfect God be anything but perfect herself?). I believed that if I could find a mistake somewhere in her writings—even one—the prophetic gift would have been nullified. After all, how could a prophet ever be wrong, especially about anything religious?

This source of this mistaken belief, I think, goes back to the definition of a "prophet." Though no one specifically taught me how inspiration works (especially hers), I made certain assumptions based on my understanding of the word "prophet." Among other things, these assumptions included the notion of "inerrancy." Where that idea came from, I don't know, though there is, I think, a tendency to automatically identify the attributes of God with those of His servants, especially those who serve Him in a prophetic role.

About a year later another incident shook up my paradigm. I read where Ellen White talked about the "reform dress," and how she was shown *in vision* what that dress should be like:

> Three companies of females passed before me, with their dresses as follows with respect to length: The first were of fashionable length, burdening the limbs, impeding the step, and sweeping the street and gathering its filth; the evil results of which I have fully stated. This class, who were slaves to fashion, appeared feeble and languid.
>
> The dress of the second class which passed before me was in many respects as it should be. The limbs were well clad. They were free from the burdens which the tyrant, Fashion, had imposed upon the first class; but had gone to that extreme in the short dress as to disgust and prejudice good people, and destroy in a great measure their own influence. This is the style and influence of the "American Costume," taught and worn by many at "Our Home," Dansville, N.Y. It does not reach to the knee. I need not say that this style of dress was shown me to be too short.
>
> A third class passed before me with cheerful countenances, and free, elastic step. Their dress was the length I have described as proper, modest, and healthful. It cleared the filth of the street and

sidewalk a few inches under all circumstances, such as ascending and descending steps, et cetera. As I have before stated, the length was not given me in inches.[1]

To me, it was perfectly clear: the Creator of the universe had shown His prophet *in vision* ("three companies of females passed before me") what the correct length of women's dresses should be. How could there ever be any question again in any faithful Adventist's mind? Yahweh had spoken, and what does the Lord speak other than absolute, irrefutable, and terminal truth?

However, at some point later, still in my Adventist nascence, I read the following from Ellen White:

> The question may be asked: "Why has this dress been laid aside, and for what reason has dress reform ceased to be advocated?" The reason for this change I will here briefly state. While many of our sisters accepted this reform from principle, others opposed the simple, healthful style of dress which it advocated. It required much labor to introduce this reform among our people. It was not enough to present before our sisters the advantages of such a dress and to convince them that it would meet the approval of God. Fashion had so strong a hold upon them that they were slow to break away from its control, even to obey the dictates of reason and conscience. And many who professed to accept the reform made no change in their wrong habits of dress, except in shortening the skirts and clothing the limbs.
>
> Nor was this all. Some who adopted the reform were not content to show by example the advantages of the dress, giving, when asked, their reasons for adopting it, and letting the matter rest there. They sought to control others' conscience by their own. If they wore it, others must put it on. They forgot that none were to be compelled to wear the reform dress.
>
> It was not my duty to urge the subject upon my sisters. After presenting it before them as it had been shown me, I left them to their own conscience. . . . Much unhappy feeling was created by those who were constantly urging the reform dress upon their sisters. With extremists, this reform seemed to constitute the sum and substance of their religion. It was the theme of conversation and the burden of their hearts; and their minds were thus diverted from

God and the truth. . . . Some were greatly troubled because I did not make the dress a test question, and still others because I advised those who had unbelieving husbands or children not to adopt the reform dress, as it might lead to unhappiness that would counteract all the good to be derived from its use. For years I carried the burden of this work and labor to establish uniformity of dress among our sisters. . . . I had no burden of testimony on the subject of dress.[2]

What?

The Creator of the universe showed her what the dress should be, but Ellen White "had no burden of testimony on the subject of dress"—even telling the women to forget it? Though I went through this experience a long time ago and don't remember my specific thoughts at the time, I do remember realizing that I had much to learn about the meaning, authority, and role of the prophetic gift.[3]

Soon after this, Brother Walter Rea made a grand debut with his accusations against Ellen White, culminating in *The White Lie*.[4] However bitter his attitude, and however much I rejected his conclusions, Rea did force the issue of her inspiration into the open. Although I didn't know about Ellen White's literary borrowings and had been an Adventist only a few months, I wasn't shocked or, as I think back, surprised. I was a little annoyed that I hadn't been told about her borrowings (and wondered what else was out there), but I soon realized that the issue of her using other sources wasn't anything new. Perhaps, the reason no one told me was because I never asked. I had never been explicitly taught that every word Ellen White wrote came directly from God as if dictated by Him; I think I just assumed that's how it happened. Plus, I was around people who used her writings as if every word were, indeed, verbally inspired. But because "we can do nothing against the truth, but for the truth" (2 Corinthians 13:8), Rea's material, by shoving these issues into the face of the church, ultimately has helped me, and others, better understand how inspiration works.

To begin, I now understand that not every statement, every word, every utterance of Ellen White is an eternal, terminal truth, the final word on any subject, be it eggs, cheese, or the "daily." And though it has never been the official church position that her every word is the final word on any subject, many Adventists still adhere to such a view either openly or obliquely. No doubt thousands are no longer among us because, having held that view, they were shattered when they discovered how untenable it is.

Much of what Ellen White wrote, whether directly from God in vision, a general sermon at a camp meeting, or a letter to a wayward member, must be placed in context. This is crucial, for it can help us understand why in one place in her writings she would strongly warn against eating eggs, while in another place she could strongly advocate eating them,[5] or why in one place she would write that "cheese is still more objectionable; it is wholly unfit for food," while in another say, "Tea, coffee, tobacco, and alcohol we must present as sinful indulgences. We cannot place on the same ground, meat, eggs, butter, cheese, and such articles placed upon the table. . . . The poisonous narcotics are not to be treated in the same way as the subject of eggs, butter, and cheese."[6]

If these specific statements are terminal truths, Yahweh's eternal commands, then there's a problem, because these eternal, terminal truths are pitted against each other. Which of these eternal, terminal truths is the ultimate eternal, terminal truth? Did God at one point forbid cheese, and then at another point change His mind making it as benign as milk and butter? Unless we allow ourselves some contextualization in how we interpret her writings, what can people do with statements like these, and others, which many view not only as direct verbal inspiration from the Lord, but as absolute truths for which there is no higher source of authority?

The key with Ellen White, I've learned, is to look at the big picture. What are the central issues she is addressing? What are the principles behind what she's saying? What is the context? It's so crucial, too, to survey all that she says on a topic, and not just pull a quote from here and there. If we focus on minors, we're going to run into various "contradictions" that demand the most convoluted and sophistic logic to solve. But above these "minor" things an incredible underlying harmony pervades her writings; the broad and important truths of salvation come out over and over again, expressed in marvelous ways. The worst thing we can do (as many have done and still do) is to build entire theologies, or even lifestyle paradigms, around a statement here and there, as if each quote were in itself absolute truth. She didn't stand for it in her life, and we defile her legacy by doing it now.

In my early Adventist years, for instance, I saw her statement about cheese being wholly "unfit for food" as a direct command from the Lord. (No one ever showed me the other quote, which placed cheese in the same category as milk and butter.) I was heavily influenced by people who practically built a lifestyle and theology around not eating cheese because of that one quote. To me, eating cheese was almost the equivalent of receiving the mark of the beast. In fact, later on, a person I was working with had to call me into her office and read some counsel from Ellen White about moderation in health reform—after which, she kindly but firmly said, "Cliff, please stop telling my staff that they will go to hell because they eat cheese!"

Later, after I loosened up some, I went out to eat with some people who ordered a pizza. I ate it, but I refused to ask God's blessing on it. *How could I ask the Lord to bless what He, through His servant, had said was wholly "unfit for food"?*

Imagine, though, my thoughts when a year or two later I read that other statement of Ellen White's (which, as I said, had not been shown me before) in which the dreaded and evil cheese was placed in the same category as milk, butter, and eggs! My head spun. What was going on here?

The problem, I then started to understand, wasn't with Ellen White, but with my understanding of her ministry. As I look at it now, trying to discern the principle here, I understand that without question Ellen White viewed cheese as unhealthy. And she was right. I just saw in *Newsweek* one of these food pyramids and, up near the top, among the foods that should be taken in small doses, if at all, was cheese. Though cheese isn't the best food (and I assume those with certain health problems should never eat it), avoiding it isn't an issue of eternal truth in the sense that eating a slice of pizza is a violation of a command of Yahweh. Especially as I age (I'm heading toward the back door of my 40s), I eat cheese less and less. But it says a lot about how thoroughly we've messed up this Ellen White thing that it took me years to get to the point that I didn't feel like I needed to be re-baptized because I ate a slice of brie!

I realize now how ludicrous and untenable my early views were. I'm so thankful that, early on, I began seeing things differently, before having years, even decades, of misunderstandings to undo. The clay was reconfigured while still soft. Try remodeling hard clay; it crumbles into pieces that are easily blown away by any breeze, with nothing but empty pews remaining.

How did we get ourselves in this mess? I don't know. Ever since the Lord gave us the prophetic gift through the ministry of Ellen White, we've struggled to know how to understand and utilize it. If Ellen White herself had to deal with those who misused and misunderstood her work and writings while she lived, what makes us think that the church would get it right long after she's gone? I don't believe anyone meant ill, but we've created something that's proving difficult to tame. After Ellen White's death, some of those seeking to defend this wonderful gift perhaps went too far, creating an edifice that was built on shaky pillars, an edifice that was not needed to begin with, one that has now created many more problems than it has solved. Worse than not defending the gift is defending it with weak arguments. We'd have been better off keeping silent than speaking things that weren't correct.

For worship, I've been reading the first five books of Moses in my Hebrew Bible and then reading *Patriarch and Prophets*. One morning as I was reading, it hit me: *Maybe we should have just left her alone.* That is, instead of building this entire apologetic structure, maybe we should have said little, instead letting the material speak for itself. Rather than cram it down people's throats, maybe we should have just printed the books, sold them cheaply, and sat back and let the Holy Spirit—who no doubt worked through the writer—work through the reader.

Though it's too late to turn back, much can still be done. Before anyone joins this church, George Knight's *Reading Ellen White*[7] ought to be requisite study material. Knight captures the essence of the issue regarding her inspiration. He covers many topics—everything from her role in theology, to her use of historical sources, to her relationship to the Bible, as well as her *fallibility*. Maybe I'm naive, but if this book, or one like it, would have been written at the beginning of the twentieth century, rather than at the end, we wouldn't be in the situation we're in now, and thousands who left because they didn't understand her ministry would still be here, including, maybe, Brother Ratzlaff.

## BROTHER DALE AND ELLEN WHITE

Which brings us back to *The Cultic Doctrine of Seventh-day Adventists*, Brother Ratzlaff's polemic against the pre-Advent judgment, even though most of the book is an attack on Ellen White's prophetic ministry.

As I said earlier, if he could disprove the pre-Advent judgment, Ellen White would be a moot point. But, as we have seen, his "biblical evaluation" of the doctrine turned out to be as paltry as, for instance, his pointing to *The Study Bible* as proof that Adventists are "tampering with the Word." Even if the pre-Advent judgment were not biblical, it would still take something better than his rehash of the same old arguments—not to mention his complete ignoring of the church's best defenses against those arguments—in order to show that it's not.

His attacks on Ellen White are of the same caliber as his attack on the pre-Advent judgment—rehashed material, a selective use of the facts, ignoring of our best defenses, etc. I usually don't get apologetic about Ellen White; there's no need to. Her ministry speaks for itself. Plus, as I've said, and repeat because it's crucial: I don't need her. I know what I need to know to be an Adventist Christian from my Bible. Thus, his attack on Ellen White, even if valid, disproves none of our doctrines (even Brother Dale admits that "Ellen White never originated a single doctrine of Adventism"[8]). Nevertheless, because this book is a response to his, I would be remiss in not looking at least some of his charges against her.

In the preface, Brother Dale, writing about himself and his wife, says, "We both accepted the writings of Ellen G. White as inspired and authoritative."[9]

That's fine; I and millions of others do, too. But what does he mean by "inspired"? Inerrancy? Immutability? Verbal inspiration? It becomes clear as you read his book that these attributes are exactly what he means. Also, what does he mean by "authoritative"? He explains that himself: "However, having grown up on SDA church history and having once accepted the writings of EGW on an equal authority with the Bible. . . ."[10] Elsewhere he writes, "I accepted her writings on an equal authority with the Bible for many years of my life."[11]

Again, in fairness to Brother Dale, he got those views honestly. Whatever position we may take officially as a church, there are a lot of Adventists who hold the same sentiments as he did. No wonder he, and others, had problems. It's hard to see how anyone couldn't.

With this in mind, we can better understand the nature of his attack because it stems from erroneous presuppositions regarding Ellen White's inspiration and authority. No matter how good your logic, if your presuppositions are wrong, you're likely to get wrong conclusions. Brother Dale is a prime example.

## ELLEN WHITE AND WILLIAM MILLER

In what is the crux of his attack, Brother Dale goes on for pages about "Ellen White's comprehensive endorsement of William Miller's methods and message."[12] He pursues this point vigorously, because he believes he has found in it the key to debunk her ministry. His logic is as follows: Ellen White, through her visions, endorsed William Miller. Miller had errors. Ellen White, therefore, can't be a true prophet.

Now, as we look at her endorsement of William Miller, and at Brother Dale's critique of that endorsement, remember this point: Everything Ellen White wrote about Miller and about God guiding Miller, she wrote *after the 1844 disappointment.* In other words, everything she's saying she said after Christ had not returned in 1843 or 1844, when Miller had expected Him to. Though Brother Dale acknowledges this fact,[13] he ignores its implications because, to a great degree, they gut the force of his case.

Think about it. Ellen White wrote about Miller after 1844, after the Disappointment, after it was obvious that in *some* things at least, Miller was wrong. The main expected event, the Second Coming, didn't happen, and Ellen White knew it didn't. How comprehensive, then, was her "comprehensive endorsement"? Obviously, it didn't include everything Miller taught, not even the most important point, because she knew that Christ hadn't returned in 1843 or 1844. If she had been shown in vision beforehand that one or the other date was correct, then it might be a different story. But whatever else she endorsed about Miller, she did knowing full well (after all, she had experienced the Great Disappointment herself) that Miller had been wrong about the Second Coming at least.

Thus, right out of the gate, Brother Dale is confronted with a dilemma whose implications he studiously ignores. The timing of her writing proves that whatever she endorsed about Miller, it wasn't as "comprehensive" as Brother Dale claims, if by "comprehensive" he means everything Miller taught. Obviously, at the time of her writing, she didn't endorse his claim that Christ would return in 1843-1844. And once you acknowledge that her endorsement didn't cover everything Miller taught, the argument changes. Now, one has to sift through the material and see just what it was she did and did not endorse, something Brother Dale, in his sweeping charges against her, doesn't do, at least not overtly.

Indeed, as we saw in chapter 1 (but worth repeating), Brother Dale spends enormous energy on Miller's fifteen "proofs" for 1844, the idea being that Ellen White endorsed all these and therefore can't be a prophet. Yet in a later footnote (a footnote!) He admits that "it's not clear if Ellen White endorsed all of Miller's fifteen 'proofs.' "[14]

Look at what's happening. Brother Dale expounds page after page on the silliness of Miller's proofs, arguing that because Ellen White endorsed them she cannot be a prophet. *And yet, later, he admits that maybe she didn't endorse them all!* Thus, if "it's not clear if Ellen White endorsed all of Miller's fifteen 'proofs,' " then it's not clear that her "comprehensive endorsement" of Miller is as comprehensive as Brother Dale needs it to be in order to build his case against her.

In fact, nowhere in *CDSDA* does Brother Dale give an example of Ellen White endorsing Miller's other "proofs" for 1843-1844 (apart from the argument based on Daniel 8:14), be they from Ezekiel, the Levitical jubilees, or Exodus. Even one example would have provided powerful evidence to buttress his polemic, yet he presents nothing because he has nothing. Contrary to the point upon which he builds an entire argument against Ellen White (that she endorsed *all* these proofs), no evidence indicates that she ever accepted any of Miller's other evidences as valid time prophecies that would end in 1843-1844.

Read *The Great Controversy.* What does she use to establish 1844? Levitical jubilees, Ezekiel 39:9, 10; Exodus 31:13-17, or some of Miller's other texts? No, she uses only one—Daniel 8:14, the one Brother Dale tried so hard, and failed, to refute.

So far, we've established that however "comprehensive" her endorsement of Miller, it certainly didn't include his belief that Christ would return in 1843-1844 (arguably the most important part of his message), nor, despite his claims, has Brother Dale produced one example of her endorsing any of Miller's other fourteen "proofs" for 1844 apart from Daniel 8:14.

Let's go further. Brother Dale quotes Ellen White's words about the involvement of angels in Miller's ministry such as, "Angels of God repeatedly visited that chosen one [Miller], and guided his mind, and opened his understanding to prophecies which had been ever dark to God's people."[15] He also notes that she wrote that the Lord had been leading Miller and that "God led the mind of Miller into the prophecies, and gave him great light upon the book of Revelation."[16]

How could angels, or even God, be guiding Miller if his positions contained errors? And yet, Ellen White endorsed him, even with his errors. She, therefore, had to be a false prophet.

Brother Dale's thinking, however logical, begins with a false premise, that those whom God or angels lead must be theologically infallible. He's fallen into the trap mentioned earlier: the understandable tendency to equate the attributes of God with His messengers.

For instance, God led John the Baptist. After all, Jesus Himself said that there was no greater prophet than John (Luke 7:28). And yet, we find John questioning the Messiahship of Jesus (Matthew 11:3), no small theological point, to be sure. Or what about Peter who, though certainly led of God, refused to eat with Gentiles when other Jews were around (Galatians 2)? Thus, sometime after the Cross, after Jesus told Peter to "feed my sheep" (John 21:17), after even Pentecost, Peter seems to have missed one of the foundational truths of what Jesus taught and what the Cross was to accomplish (Galatians 3:28).

In *The Great Controversy*, Ellen White wrote of Martin Luther that "angels of heaven were by his side, and rays of light from the throne of God revealed the treasure of truth to his understanding."[17] Does that mean that everything Luther wrote was from God? What Protestant who loves the gospel that Martin Luther unearthed from centuries of rubbish and superstition doesn't believe that the Lord led Luther? And yet, did Ellen White's endorsement (after all having angels of heaven by your side is a pretty good endorsement) mean that she would have supported Luther's vitriol against those who believed in the seventh-day Sabbath? Would she have endorsed his attacks against Ulrich Zwingli, who argued that the bread and wine in the Lord's Supper were just symbols as opposed to Luther's more Catholic-leaning position of a real presence of Christ in them? Did this mean that she agreed with Luther's diatribes against the Jews, in which he wrote things the Nazis used centuries later to help pave the way for mass murder? Yet, to follow Brother Dale's logic, since angels from heaven were sent to Luther and he was led of God, therefore, how could he be in error? In the same way, angels of God guided Miller, who was led of God; therefore how could he be in error?

Knowing the context of Miller's (and Ellen White's) religious world is crucial in understanding her endorsement. Miller preached during an era of rampant postmillennialism. Protestants believed that Christ would return *after* the millennium on earth, a millennium that they believed the world was now entering. The world, they taught, would steadily improve until it reached a state of utopia, at which time Jesus would return and assume His throne in Jerusalem. Darwin, meanwhile, publishing his material on evolution—which argued that humans themselves were evolving toward a higher state—added his own fuel to the postmillennialist fire. This postmillennial doctrine was held by millions of Protestants into the first few decades of the twentieth, and was dislodged only by World War I.

But more than half a century before the Somme and Verdun, Miller's Advent message unabashedly railed against this silliness. Studying the prophecies of Daniel and Revelation, Miller—led of God and His angels—said *No, No, No, the world isn't getting better. On the contrary, it's getting worse, and it's heading not toward some earthly millennial paradise but toward a final cataclysm that will end with the return of Christ.* It was this basic teaching, in the context of Miller's calculations around the time prophecies of Daniel 8 and 9, as opposed to postmillennialism, that Ellen White endorsed—just as she endorsed Luther's basic teaching on the gospel and justification by faith in the context of opposition to the whole papal system. Her endorsement no more covered all that Miller taught than it covered all that Luther taught. In both cases, she pulled out a basic thread, or flow of belief, and concentrated on that.

Brother Dale runs with these two statements: "I saw that God was in the proclamation of the time in 1843. It was His design to arouse the people and bring them to a testing point, where they should decide for or against the truth"[18] and, "I have seen that the 1843 chart was directed by the hand of the Lord, and that it should not be altered; that the figures were as He wanted them; that His hand was over and hid a mistake in some of the figures, so that none could see it, until His hand was removed."[19]

Again, she wrote this *after* the 1844 disappointment, so she knew that not everything Miller taught was correct, particularly the 1843 date. Indeed, despite Brother Dale's claim about her "comprehensive" endorsement, she says right in the quotation he cites that some of the figures in Miller's chart were wrong—more proof that her endorsement of Miller didn't cover everything. Thus, besides knowing (obviously) that Miller was wrong about the event in 1844, she knew he had some of the figures wrong, too. Hardly a blanket endorsement, to be sure.

But what is she talking about? Did God purposely deceive the Millerites by holding His hand over error?

To begin, we're dealing with a metaphor here (God's hand covering mistakes in Miller's chart), and metaphors are just that, metaphors, and thus not to be taken literally. I see two possible approaches here:

1. God supernaturally hid the truth from Miller and his followers, much as Jesus did with the men on the road to Emmaus (Luke 24:13-16).

2. God didn't reveal more truth to Miller at that time, despite some errors in his thinking, just as He didn't reveal more truth to the disciples who asked just before Jesus returned to heaven, "Lord, wilt thou at this time restore again the kingdom to Israel?" (Acts 1:6.)

I opt for the second approach—that the Lord simply took Miller and his followers as far as they were able to go at that time, a principle seen in various places in the Bible as well (1 Corinthians 3:2; John 16:12). One of the clearest examples is with the woman at the well in John 4. Why did Jesus tell her, a non-Jew, that He was the Messiah, when with the Jews He wasn't so candid? It's because the Lord knew just how far people could be led, how far their minds could be stretched with truths that they didn't fully understand.

And this, I believe, explains what's happening here. The Lord took Miller and others as far as they were able to go *at that time*. That's why Ellen

White could write that the figures were just as God wanted them, *at that time*, and that nothing was to be altered, *at that time*. (Remember, she was writing this after it was clear that the 1843 figure was wrong.) Then, when the time was right, the Lord removed His hand, that is, He gave His people more light, and they could see their mistakes.

In the late 1970s, the Lord used a book written by Hal Lindsey to help open me up to the truth of Christianity. Though filled with one ridiculous teaching after another, the book was, nevertheless, a catalyst that helped bring me to Christ. Over time I saw the errors, even though the Lord had used those errors, *at that time*, to take me from where I was to where He eventually wanted me to be.

It's also important to know that Ellen White wrote what she did about the 1843 date in the context of those who were setting other, later, dates. Trying to get them away from date setting, she affirmed the basic calculations of Miller, which despite some errors, were essentially right.

Brother Dale makes a big deal out of the fact that she said the Lord was "in the proclamation of 1843." But how could He be because, after all, the proclamation contained error? Again, could God not be leading people who still had some error? Luther is a prime example. Also, I believe the Lord has led the Seventh-day Adventist Church, even though some among us in the early years held errors—for instance, non-Trinitarian views. God took the Millerites as far as they were able to go at that time. If you believe, as I do, that Miller's basic calculations regarding Daniel 8 and 9 were correct, despite a mistake in "some of the figures," then it's quite amazing how far God had led them, allowing them to get so much truth from the Bible, especially at a time when the prevailing theological currents were teaching that the world had already entered a glorious thousand-year period that would climax with Jesus ruling the happy planet from Jerusalem.

Again, if the 1844 judgment is wrong, it's going to take a lot more evidence than Brother Dale has presented to prove it wrong. But it's right; God *did* lead Miller and there *were* angels at his side. God used Miller to lay the foundation of the Seventh-day Adventist Church, which paved the way for the modern eschatological platform held by so many Christian denominations today, which thanks to Adventists includes the idea of a visible second coming of Christ at the end of the world.

Then there are the three angels' messages of Revelation 14, the most rational, historically valid, and theologically balanced understanding of last-day events that has ever been developed. (What are some of the alternatives? How about, for instance, the secret rapture—in which airline pilots disappear from the cockpit, swept up to heaven, with nothing remaining behind but their uniforms?) Seventh-day Adventists are the largest non-Jewish Sabbath-keeping movement in the world and is one of the few Christian denominations that has shed the Greek concept of an immortal soul and the pagan idea of the righteous dead going right to heaven, a "baptized" version of Plato's ascent of the soul. And despite Brother Dale's failed attempt to debunk it, the 1844 pre-Advent judgment is the final heavenly event (see Daniel 7) that leads to the Second Coming and the end of the world; thus it's an event of massive importance that Adventists alone are teaching. All this, and more, began with William Miller. No wonder Ellen White endorsed him.

Let's review:

- Ellen White knew that Miller was wrong about the event itself, the Second Coming in 1844, because she wrote after the Disappointment.
- Brother Dale is forced to admit that it's not clear that she endorsed all of Miller's proofs.
- Brother Dale gives no example of her ever endorsing any of Miller's arguments other than his proof from Daniel 8:14 (and that's because she didn't do so).
- Despite her statements that God led Miller, that's no proof that she endorsed everything Miller taught.
- She even admitted that there was a mistake in some of Miller's figures.

Brother Dale builds one of his main arguments against Ellen White on the premise of her "comprehensive" endorsement of Miller and all that he taught. The evidence proves that premise wrong; his argument, therefore, fails.

## THE SHUT DOOR

No one attacking Ellen White ever avoids opening the "shut door" controversy. This issue began early in her ministry and, no matter the evidence countering the critics' conclusions, is still brought up because of a few lines that—taken out of context and without explanation—make good fodder for the critics.

I don't intend to repeat all that's been written on this (and much has). Instead, I want to look at the main accusation, which is that Ellen White was shown *in vision* that the door of mercy had shut on the whole world after 1844. Then I want to ask, What evidence does Brother Dale present to prove that accusation?

Notice, the question is *not:* Did Ellen White ever *believe* that the door of probation had closed for the world after 1844? She, along with many of the Millerites, did believe this, at least for a while, even after she started having visions. But holding a belief is a different issue entirely than the claim that she was shown in vision that the whole world was lost after 1844. After all, having a vision doesn't suddenly make a person infallible in all her knowledge.

Brother Dale seeks to discredit Ellen White. And if having ever held an erroneous view, even after receiving the prophetic gift, is all that it takes to discredit her, the battle's over before it's fought. But his argument (and that of others) is that she was shown in vision, by God, that probation for the whole world had ended after 1844.

Brother Dale quotes material from the Camden vision, which has long been suspect as a fraud, so we can discard that. Let's go, instead, with what is unquestionably her authentic writings. Interestingly enough, Brother Dale produces nothing in which Ellen White says that the Lord or an angel showed her in vision that probation had closed for the world after 1844. Instead, he takes a quote from one of her early visions and builds his case mostly from it.

The quote in question is from her first vision which was given to her on December 1844:

> While praying at the family altar, the Holy Ghost fell on me, and I seemed to be rising higher and higher, far above the dark world. I turned to look for the Advent people in the world, but could not find them—when a voice said to me, "Look again, and look a little higher." At this I raised my eyes and saw a straight and narrow path, cast up high above the world. On this path the Advent people were traveling to the City, which was at the farther end of the path. They had a bright light set up behind them at the first end of the path, which an angel told me was the Midnight Cry. This light shone all along the path, and gave light for their feet so they might not stumble. And if they kept their eyes fixed on Jesus, who was just before them, leading them to the City, they were safe. But soon some grew weary, and they said the City was a great way off, and they expected to have entered it before. Then Jesus would encourage them by raising his glorious right arm, and from his arm came a glorious light which waved over the Advent band, and they shouted Hallelujah! *Others rashly denied the light behind them, and said that it*

*was not God that had led them out so far. The light behind them went out leaving their feet in perfect darkness, and they stumbled and got their eyes off the mark and lost sight of Jesus, and fell off the path down in the dark and wicked world below. It was just as impossible for them to get on the path again and go to the City, as all the wicked world which God had rejected* [20] (italics supplied).

Brother Ratzlaff quotes this part of this vision, and writes, "EGW was shown that it was impossible for the people who renounced the Millerite message, or its interpretation, to be saved. Second, God had rejected *all* the wicked world."[21]

There are a few problems, however, with his interpretation of what the vision says. To begin, read what she wrote—or didn't write. She never said that *she was shown* that the whole wicked world was lost. Never did she say, "An angel showed me that the whole wicked world was lost," or "The Lord showed me that the whole wicked world was lost"—the kind of language she used in numerous other instances. That she might have *believed* these things, at least for a while, is another matter. At most, what happened here is that she *might* have read some things into her *interpretation* of the vision which were not specifically taught by the vision. And whatever questions that suggestion might evoke, it's not the same as saying that she had been shown this belief by God.

The above quote was taken from her first vision, given when she was a seventeen-year-old girl, not highly educated, not overly literate, nor well-read nor theologically sophisticated. That she could have read more into the vision than was warranted, or even that she might have misinterpreted the vision—particularly since it was her first one—is far different from specifically saying that she was shown something by God. Years later she would write: "Often representations are given me which at first I do not understand, but after a time they are made plain by a repeated presentation of those things that I did not at first comprehend, and in ways that make their meaning clear and unmistakable" (Letter 329, 1904). So even after experiencing the prophetic gift for a number of years, she says that sometimes she doesn't understand at first what is shown her, and only later, by repeated presentations, does she finally understand. Daniel, likewise, said that he didn't understand the vision of the 2,300 days (Daniel 8:27), and it wasn't until years later that more information was given to him (see Daniel 9:24-27).

Thus, whatever Ellen White was shown in that first vision, she could have simply read more into it than was there. Is that not possible for a prophet to do, or are we again attributing the attributes of Deity to His prophets?

But couldn't God have rearranged the neurons in her brain so she would have interpreted the vision perfectly? Of course He could, in the same way He could have rearranged the neurons in John the Baptist's head so that he would not have doubted the Messiahship of Jesus. Why God didn't do so in either case is, I suppose, a question that we can one day ask Him face to face. Meanwhile, we're left with the idea that Ellen Harmon, this seventeen-year-old girl, given her first vision, might simply have used language descriptive of beliefs that she already held when first given the vision.

Ellen White (then Harmon) along with the Millerites believed that when Christ would return, the door of probation would be closed, much like we believe today. After Christ didn't return, many of these Millerites still clung to some of their beliefs surrounding the events of 1844, including the idea that sinners had rejected their day of grace in 1844.

However, correcting this error was not the purpose of that first vision. Instead, the Lord wanted to show Ellen White that the Millerites shouldn't give up on their Advent faith, that God had led them, and that they needed to stay on the path and not fall away like others who had rejected the light God had given. That's the point of the vision: to keep the Millerites from turning away, as others had done.

Then there's the whole question of the grammatical construction of the last clause in that final sentence, which reads, "as all the wicked world which God had rejected." The grammar is ambiguous; it can be understood in either a restrictive or nonrestrictive manner, with two entirely different meanings.

Read the following two sentences:
- *The house that is red burned down.*
- *The house, which is red, burned down.*

The difference isn't readily apparent, but they're not saying the same thing. Grammatically, the first sentence (which is nonrestrictive) implies the existence of two or more houses, one of which happens to be red. It is that house—the red one—that burned. The second sentence (which is restrictive) implies there is only one house, and that house is red.

When you read the clause that Ellen White wrote, "all the wicked world which God had rejected," the grammar isn't clear whether "which God had rejected" is a restrictive clause or a nonrestrictive one. In other words, did she mean that all the world was wicked, and God had rejected it all (nonrestrictive)? Or did she mean that God had rejected only the wicked people in the world, but not those in the world who were not wicked (restrictive)? If it's the latter, then the issue at stake isn't even a question of interpretation but of grammar, which shouldn't be a problem unless folks believe that God's perfection and infallibility must be present in the grammar of His servants as well.

Years later, responding to charges that she had taught through her visions that probation had closed for the world in 1844 (and therefore that these statements had been left out of later printings of the visions), Ellen White wrote:

> It is claimed that these expressions prove the shut-door doctrine, and that this is the reason of their omission in later editions. But in fact they teach only that which has been and is still held by us as a people, as I shall show.
>
> For a time after the disappointment in 1844, I did hold, in common with the advent body, that the door of mercy was then forever closed to the world. This position was taken before my first vision was given me. It was the light given me of God that corrected our error, and enabled us to see the true position.

Notice, she's saying very clearly that, prior to her first vision, she believed as did other Adventists that the door of mercy was forever closed. She's *not* saying that her first vision corrected that view, only that she held this view *prior* to her first vision. Later, gradually, from light given to her of God after the first vision, her position changed. The first vision was given for another purpose, even if she possibly read more into it than the Lord intended. She continued her explanation:

> I am still a believer in the shut-door theory, but not in the sense in which we at first employed the term or in which it is employed by my opponents.
>
> There was a shut door in Noah's day. There was at that time a withdrawal of the Spirit of God from the sinful race that perished in the waters of the Flood. God Himself gave the shut-door message to Noah: "My spirit shall not always strive with man, for that he also is flesh: yet his days shall be an hundred and twenty years" (Gen. 6:3).

There was a shut door in the days of Abraham. Mercy ceased to plead with the inhabitants of Sodom, and all but Lot, with his wife and two daughters, were consumed by the fire sent down from heaven.

There was a shut door in Christ's day. The Son of God declared to the unbelieving Jews of that generation, "Your house is left unto you desolate" (Matt. 23:38).

Looking down the stream of time to the last days, the same infinite power proclaimed through John: "These things saith he that is holy, he that is true, he that hath the key of David, he that openeth, and no man shutteth; and shutteth, and no man openeth" (Rev. 3:7).

I was shown in vision, and I still believe, that there was a shut door in 1844. All who saw the light of the first and second angels' messages and rejected that light, were left in darkness. And those who accepted it and received the Holy Spirit which attended the proclamation of the message from heaven, and who afterward renounced their faith and pronounced their experience a delusion, thereby rejected the Spirit of God, and it no longer pleaded with them.

Those who did not see the light, had not the guilt of its rejection. It was only the class who had despised the light from heaven that the Spirit of God could not reach. And this class included, as I have stated, both those who refused to accept the message when it was presented to them, and also those who, having received it, afterward renounced their faith. These might have a form of godliness, and profess to be followers of Christ; but having no living connection with God, they would be taken captive by the delusions of Satan. These two classes are brought to view in the vision—those who declared the light which they had followed a delusion, and the wicked of the world who, having rejected the light, had been rejected of God. No reference is made to those who had not seen the light, and therefore were not guilty of its rejection.[22]

Notice, she's taking the restrictive view, that is, she's saying that the vision did not mean that the whole world was wicked and was lost (though she herself believed that for a time), but that all those in the wicked world who, *having rejected the light*, had been rejected of God. The group rejected by God becomes, then, not the whole world, but just those who had rejected the light God had given them. And if even that seems unduly harsh, read what the author of Hebrews says in a much broader context than what Ellen White was dealing with: "For it is impossible for those who were once enlightened, and have tasted of the heavenly gift, and were made partakers of the Holy Ghost, and have tasted the good word of God, and the powers of the world to come, If they shall fall away, to renew them again unto repentance; seeing they crucify to themselves the Son of God afresh, and put him to an open shame" (Hebrews 6:4-6).

So what does the evidence indicate thus far?

First, nowhere does Ellen White ever claim to have been shown in vision that probation had closed for the entire world after 1844. Yet this is what Brother Dale claims, and he bases another attack against her on this premise.

Second, at worst one could say she read more into her first vision than was there. If someone believes that a prophet can't do that, then there is no point in arguing the point further. However, if one believes, as she herself said, that she didn't always understand at first what was shown her in vision, then the issue becomes less problematic. She simply wrote out the vision she had seen in the context of what she believed at the time. Later, over time, the Lord corrected the erroneous Millerite views.

Third, the grammar of the highly contested clause is, itself, ambiguous; it's possible to read it in a manner that doesn't mean the whole world was lost, but only a restricted part of that world. Ellen White, writing later about her views, seems to have interpreted that sentence in a manner that doesn't have her saying what her opponents claim it's saying. Thus, the critic's charge is greatly weakened, for not only did she never claim that God showed her in vision that the entire world was lost after 1844, but she later maintained that she never said it herself, whatever she might have personally believed.

Whether it's an interpretation problem or a grammatical one, either way Brother Dale's point—that she claimed in vision God showed her that probation closed for the world after 1844—is wrong.

Brother Dale also accuses the early Adventists of deception because over time they redefined their understanding of the "shut door," changing it from the idea of the close of probation to the idea of Christ's ministry in the heavenly sanctuary. To quote Ellen White again: "I am still a believer in the shut-door theory, but not in the sense in which we at first employed the term or in which it is employed by my opponents." In other words, the early Adventists learned more, they had outgrown some early errors, and now they understood the concept of the "shut door" differently than in the past. What a horrible deception!

Here's how she later used the term:

> Sabbath, March 24, 1849, we had a sweet and very interesting meeting with the brethren at Topsham, Maine. The Holy Ghost was poured out upon us, and I was taken off in the Spirit to the city of the living God. Then I was shown that the commandments of God and the testimony of Jesus Christ relating to the shut door could not be separated, and that the time for the commandments of God to shine out with all their importance, and for God's people to be tried on the Sabbath truth, was when the door was opened in the most holy place in the heavenly sanctuary, where the ark is, in which are contained the ten commandments. This door was not opened until the mediation of Jesus was finished in the holy place of the sanctuary in 1844. Then Jesus rose up and shut the door of the holy place, and opened the door into the most holy, and passed within the second veil, where He now stands by the ark, and where the faith of Israel now reaches.
>
> I saw that Jesus had shut the door of the holy place, and no man can open it; and that He had opened the door into the most holy, and no man can shut it; and that since Jesus has opened the door into the most holy place, which contains the ark, the commandments have been shining out to God's people, and they are being tested on the Sabbath question.[23]

Brother Dale seems to equate a change in understanding with deception. If so, what is he going to do with Peter, who until his vision (Acts 10) thought that Gentiles were unclean? If a church, or even a prophet, can't grow in understanding without being deceptive, Brother Dale would have a problem with the whole New Testament church, which Paul was constantly trying to bring into greater light. If the New Testament Christians grew in their understanding, and old teachings or beliefs were replaced by better ones, ones that reflected more truth, were they being dishonest? Or what about the Jews in the early church? These people still considered themselves Jews, only now with more light. Were these people being dishonest because their positions changed over time? According to Brother Dale, the answer must be "Yes."

Finally, Brother Dale makes an issue of the fact that the controversial part of Ellen White's explanation of the first vision was deleted when it appeared later in *Early Writings*, especially, he says, because the publishers denied any deletions. Here, too, Brother Dale can be accused of either shoddy scholarship or just plain dishonesty.

The preface of *Early Writings,* which is a reprint of a book published in 1851, makes the following claim:

> Aside from these, no changes from the original work have been made in the present edition, except the occasional employment of a new word, or a change in the construction of a sentence, to better express the idea, and no portion of the work has been omitted. No shadow of change has been made in any idea or sentiment of the original work, and the verbal changes have been made under the author's own eye, and with her full approval.[24]

Thus, according to the preface, no major change was made between the 1851 edition and its reprint, *Early Writings.* But what Brother Dale either didn't know, or neglected to mention, was that in the 1851 work itself *that controversial sentence had already been deleted.* This means that when the book was reprinted, under the title *Early Writings,* that quote was already gone. Thus, as the preface had said, no deletions occurred; the 1851 book was simply reprinted.

However, after quoting the *Early Writings* preface, which denied any deletions between it and the 1851 version, Brother Dale contrasts *Early Writings,* not with the 1851 version—the one mentioned in the preface— but with *the 1845 version,* where the quote was first printed. In other words, he compares *Early Writings* with a different version of the vision than the one referred to in the preface, giving the impression that the preface was untruthful when it wasn't.

Of course, this still leaves open the question of why the publishers made the deletion to begin with—even though that's a radically different issue from Brother Dale's false charge that they lied about it. But the deletion is not a big deal, unless you believe that everything written by someone with the prophetic gift is verbally dictated from heaven and therefore can undergo no editing or revision. This is not what Adventists claim for inspiration, and certainly not what we claim for Ellen White. From the beginning of her ministry, Ellen White's works have gone through editing, revisions, and changes, sometimes numerous times, as any informed Adventist should know. In 1858 she wrote *Spiritual Gifts,* which was revised in 1884 as *Spirit of Prophecy* Vol. 4, which was expanded again in 1888 to *The Great Controversy,* which faced another revision in 1911. Each of these versions involved deletions, additions, and revisions. That early Adventists, therefore, should take something she wrote at seventeen or eighteen years of age—something that had caused confusion, something that could be understood as stating a position they no longer believed—and edit it out in later versions is hardly part of some massive cover up, despite Brother Dale's claims to the contrary. There was no deception—at least on the Adventists' part.

## ELLEN WHITE AND THE GOSPEL

All through *The Cultic Doctrine of Seventh-day Adventists*, an underlying motif emerges: Ellen White's writings are anti-gospel and mitigate against the doctrine of justification by faith alone. We showed, in the last chapter, how false that claim is, at least in the context of the pre-Advent judgment. Even outside that context, however, Brother Dale keeps the charge coming:

> Ellen White says that we are *not* saved by faith alone.[25]

> EGW says that the imputed righteousness of Christ is not enough to save sinners.[26]

> EGW said it was the *false teachers* who claim that "Christ came to save sinners."[27]

> She will, however, often give the gospel with her right hand and then take it away with her left.[28]

> The confusion of the SDA church regarding the gospel must be placed squarely upon Ellen G. White.[29]

> As we have seen throughout this book, many of her statements are totally erroneous, and here is the important point: many of them distort, undermine or contradict the new covenant gospel of grace.[30]

How does one answer these charges?

Let's begin with a hypothetical situation. Suppose someone were to ask Ellen White, "Sister White, what must I do to have eternal life?" and she were to respond, "If you want eternal life, keep the commandments" (see Matthew 19:17). Why, I imagine Brother Dale would be indignant, using this response as more evidence that Ellen White's views "distort, undermine or contradict the new covenant gospel of grace."

Or suppose someone were to ask, "Sister White, how important is it that I get the victory over sin?" and she were to respond, "And if thy right hand offend thee, cut it off, and cast it from thee: for it is profitable for thee that one of thy members should perish, and not that thy whole body should be cast into hell" (see Matthew 5:30). Brother Dale would have another statement to prove that Ellen White was anti-gospel.

Or suppose she said, "Ye see then how that by works a man is justified, and not by faith only" (see James 2:17). Or "Little children, let no man deceive you: he that doeth righteousness is righteous, even as he [Jesus] is righteous" (1 John 3:7). It doesn't take much imagination to realize the reaction these words, were they from Ellen White, would evoke in Brother Dale. But they're from the Bible, and not just the Bible, but the New Testament and its covenant of grace.

Does the New Testament then take away with its left hand the gospel it offers with its right, as Brother Dale claims Ellen White does? Or do these New Testament quotes simply need to be looked at *in context*, in full view of its other writings in order to get the total meaning?

Of course, it's the latter, not only with the Bible but with Ellen White's writings. Her words need to be looked at in context and in full view of her other writings in order to get the true picture of what she says. Anyone can do as Brother Dale does and quote a bunch of her statements without reference to the context, without reference to other things she said, without reference to the big picture, and have her sound as legalistic or anti-gospel as do Paul, James, or even Jesus in the Bible quotes listed above.

Below are just a few Ellen White statements on the gospel. Though I'm doing what I just decried in Brother Dale (stringing together Ellen White quotes without context), I do it to show that she, just like the Bible, has some very strong statements that clearly teach justification by faith alone despite other statements that, when taken in isolation or out of the full context of her writing, can sound legalistic (as can the Bible). Here, however, are a few statements from Ellen White on the subject of salvation and justification:

There is not a point that needs to be dwelt upon more earnestly, repeated more frequently, or established more firmly in the minds of all, than the impossibility of fallen man meriting anything by his own best good works. Salvation is through faith in Jesus Christ alone. . . .

Let the subject be made distinct and plain that it is not possible to effect anything in our standing before God or in the gift of God to us through creature merit. Should faith and works purchase the gift of salvation for anyone, then the Creator is under obligation to the creature. Here is an opportunity for falsehood to be accepted as truth. If any man can merit salvation by anything he may do, then he is in the same position as the Catholic to do penance for his sins. Salvation, then, is partly of debt that may be earned as wages. If man cannot, by any of his good works, merit salvation, then it must be wholly of grace, received by man as a sinner because he receives and believes in Jesus. It is wholly a free gift. Justification by faith is placed beyond controversy. And all this controversy is ended, as soon as the matter is settled that the merits of fallen man in his good works can never procure eternal life for him.[31]

The light given me of God places this important subject above any question in my mind. Justification is wholly of grace and not procured by any works that fallen man can do. The matter has been presented before me in clear lines that if the rich man has money and possessions, and he makes an offering of the same to the Lord, false ideas come in to spoil the offering by the thought he has merited the favor of God, that the Lord is under obligation to him to regard him with special favor because of this gift.[32]

My brethren, are you expecting that your merit will recommend you to the favor of God, thinking that you must be free from sin before you trust His power to save? If this is the struggle going on in your mind, I fear you will gain no strength, and will finally become discouraged.[33]

Grace is unmerited favor, and the believer is justified without any merit of his own, without any claim to offer to God. He is justified through the redemption that is in Christ Jesus, who stands in the courts of heaven as the sinner's substitute and surety.[34]

Every soul may say: "By His perfect obedience He has satisfied the claims of the law, and my only hope is found in looking to Him as my substitute and surety, who obeyed the law perfectly for me. By faith in His merits I am free from the condemnation of the law. He clothes me with His righteousness, which answers all the demands of the law. I am complete in Him who brings in everlasting righteousness. He presents me to God in the spotless garment of which no thread was woven by any human agent. All is of Christ, and all the glory, honor, and majesty are to be given to the Lamb of God, which taketh away the sins of the world.[35]

We are accepted in the Beloved. The sinner's defects are covered by the perfection and fullness of the Lord our Righteousness. Those who with sincere will, with contrite heart, are putting forth humble efforts to live up to the requirements of God, are looked upon by the Father with pitying, tender love; He regards such as obedient children, and the righteousness of Christ is imputed unto them.[36]

I have a most earnest desire that you shall enter the city of God, not as a culprit barely pardoned, but as a conqueror.[37]

As the sinner looks to the law, his guilt is made plain to him and pressed home to his conscience, and he is condemned. His only comfort and hope is found in looking to the cross of Calvary. As he ventures upon the promises, taking God at His word, relief and peace come to his soul. He cries, "Lord, Thou hast promised to save all who come unto Thee in the name of Thy Son. I am a lost, helpless, hopeless soul. Lord, save, or I perish." His faith lays hold on Christ, and he is justified before God.[38]

By Him who speaketh truth he is declared righteous. The Lord imputes unto the believer the righteousness of Christ and pronounces him righteous before the universe. He transfers his sins to Jesus, the sinner's representative, substitute, and surety. Upon Christ He lays the iniquity of every soul that believeth. "He hath made him to be sin for us, who knew no sin; that we might be made the righteousness of God in him" (2 Corinthians 5:21).[39]

"Abraham believed God, and it was counted unto him for righteousness. Now to him that worketh is the reward not reckoned of grace, but of debt. But to him that worketh not, but believeth on him that justifieth the ungodly, his faith is counted for righteousness" (Romans 4:3-5). Righteousness is obedience to the law. The law demands righteousness, and this the sinner owes to the law; but he is incapable of rendering it. The only way in which he can attain to righteousness is through faith. By faith he can bring to God the merits of Christ, and the Lord places the obedience of His Son to the sinner's account. Christ's righteousness is accepted in place of man's failure, and God receives, pardons, justifies, the repentant, believing soul, treats him as though he were righteous, and loves him as He loves His Son. This is how faith is accounted righteousness; and the pardoned soul goes on from grace to grace, from light to a greater light.[40]

When God pardons the sinner, remits the punishment he deserves, and treats him as though he had not sinned, He receives him into divine favor, and justifies him through the merits of Christ's righteousness. The sinner can be justified only through faith in the atonement made through God's dear Son, who became a sacrifice for the sins of the guilty world. No one can be justified by any works of his own. He can be delivered from the guilt of sin, from the condemnation of the law, from the penalty of transgression, only by virtue of the suffering, death, and resurrection of Christ. Faith is the only condition upon which justification can be obtained, and faith includes not only belief but trust.[41]

And, just to set the record straight regarding Brother Dale's accusation that Ellen White didn't believe in the idea that Christ came to save sinners, here's a quote from *The Desire of Ages*:

It is thus that every sinner may come to Christ. "Not by works of righteousness which we have done, but according to His mercy He saved us." Titus 3:5. When Satan tells you that you are a sinner, and cannot hope to receive blessing from God, tell him that Christ came into the world to save sinners. We have nothing to recommend us to God; but the plea that we may urge now and ever is our utterly helpless condition that makes His redeeming power a necessity. Renouncing all self-dependence, we may look to the cross of Calvary and say,—
"In my hand no price I bring;
Simply to Thy cross I cling."[42]

For some reason, these quotes and numerous others like them, never made it into *CDSDA*. Thus, Brother Dale's accusation that Ellen White didn't believe in justification by faith alone is about as uniformed and wrong as his claim that Antiochus is the little horn of Daniel 8.

## DETRITUS

One could write a book exposing the weakness of Brother Dale's attacks on Ellen White. That's not my intention. The past few pages, I believe, have made my point: His criticisms of her and her writings are of the same caliber as his "biblical evaluation" of the pre-Advent judgment. Again, in fairness to Brother Ratzlaff, he got some of his views about Ellen White honestly, and had he properly understood her and her inspiration, I doubt he'd be where he is today.

Brother Dale makes another statement about her, the final one I'm going to look at—though many more are worth scrutiny. In reference to Ellen White having changed some of her beliefs over the years, he says, "To her credit, unlike many 'prophets' of her day, her change in doctrine was usually toward mainstream Christianity."[43] Even Kenneth Richard Samples, the Christian scholar who penned the foreword to *The Cultic Doctrine of Seventh-day Adventists*, writes, "In fact, Ellen G. White seemed to play a significant role in helping the Adventist church move toward theological orthodoxy."[44]

These are fascinating admissions, fraught with conclusions that Brother Dale doesn't work through. In his sentence he places quote marks around the word "prophets," the implication being that he questions her prophetic ministry. Fair enough. But how many other modern day "prophets" have moved their churches toward "mainstream Christianity," as Brother Dale says Ellen White did? Has Sun Myung Moon, leader of the Unification Church? Or Joseph Smith of the Mormons? Or Mary Baker Eddy of Christian Science? Please! All of these prophets, without equivocation or exception, have led their people *away* from mainstream Christianity, because they all are *false* prophets. And yet Brother Dale admits that Ellen White, one of these "prophets," moved the church toward the mainstream, or as Kenneth Samples says, toward "theological orthodoxy." That's kind of a strange thing for someone to do, who (according to Brother Dale) practiced deception, taught false doctrine, and wrote against the gospel.

Ellen White made claims about her ministry that leave no room for compromise or ambivalence about those claims. She claimed to have seen things that could have come only from supernatural inspiration. Either her claims are true or she was a lunatic and/or a powerful liar who promulgated her insane ravings or amazing deceptions from the middle of the nineteenth into the second decade of the twentieth century.

What rational options are there for someone who claimed to have seen, in vision, what she claimed to have seen? She claimed to have seen Jesus bring the redeemed into the Holy City. She claimed to have seen people living on other planets and angels protecting God's people. She claimed to have seen, in vision, Jesus in the heavenly sanctuary or what Satan looked like in heaven before he sinned. She claimed to have seen angels visiting Adam and Eve in Eden. She said that she saw the look on Adam's face when he realized that Eve had sinned. She claimed to have seen Jesus, in vision, and what His face was like after the wilderness fast. She claimed to have seen the resurrection of Jesus from the tomb, as well as an angel release Paul and Silas from prison. She claimed to have seen Satan lead lost multitudes into the final rebellion against God after the second resurrection. She claimed to have seen, in vision, life in the new earth, and on and on. . . .

What does one do with these claims? Those who place her ministry on the level, for instance, of Martin Luther, are living in a logical fantasy world. Either we take her for what she has claimed for herself (which, of course, leaves open a whole group of questions that we, as a church, haven't always answered in the most fortuitous manner), or we have to reject her as a liar, a lunatic, or someone inspired by the devil. These are the only *logical* options.

I have a friend, a former Adventist, who left the church over Ellen White and who now believes she was of the devil. (He was the one who introduced me to Brother Ratzlaff's book.) However much I disagree with his conclusion, I respect his logic. Given what we know about the scope, length, and character of her life and work, something supernatural has to be behind it. And if one rejects her ministry as being from God, then who else but the devil?

Yet, interestingly enough, despite presenting quote after quote from her pen of supposedly horrific, anti-biblical error, Brother Dale never says that she was demonic (at least, I didn't see such a statement) even though that's the only logical conclusion given the nature of his attack. Page after page he rants about her false teaching, errors, and anti-gospel beliefs. So why doesn't he simply say what should be obvious? After all, who but the devil is going to use this woman to lead millions and millions astray with false, anti-gospel doctrines that have no basis in the Bible, as Brother Dale believes she has done?

Maybe, though, Brother Dale isn't ready to follow his conclusions to the end because that conclusion doesn't fit all the facts that he's keenly aware of. Is he really ready to claim that the woman who wrote *The Desire of Ages* or *Steps to Christ* was of the devil? Having grown up in the church, maybe he knows enough about her and her life to realize just how ludicrous such a conclusion is.

However tempting to continue (there's so much more to refute), I'll stop here and conclude.

Brother Dale's book is based on proving these few points:

*1. That Ellen White endorsed all of Miller's theology.* He failed. The evidence, contrary to his claim, is clear that she *didn't* endorse all of Miller's positions.

*2. That the pre-Advent judgment in 1844 is not biblical.* He failed here too. Brother Dale will have to come up with something much more persuasive than a bunch of arthritic Des Ford arguments before proving that 1844 isn't biblical.

*3. That the pre-Advent judgment contradicts the gospel.* He failed here, even miserably. Indeed, only by understanding the judgment can one fully understand the gospel.

*4. That Ellen White's theology was contrary to the new covenant teaching of salvation by faith alone.* He failed, again. Her own words, quoted a few pages earlier, prove just how badly he failed on this point.

Yet Brother Ratzlaff's failures are our own. I'm far from excusing his actions, yet as a church we have failed to make some things—particularly the gospel-centeredness of the judgment, as well as the role and nature of Ellen White's ministry—as clear as they should be. We are now reaping the results. *The Cultic Doctrine of Seventh-day Adventists* is a prime example.

That Brother Dale's book has greatly affected some among us, and even turned them away from us, is a testimony, not to the power of his arguments but to how poorly informed many Seventh-day Adventists are. His book will influence those who, already angered, hurt, and disgruntled with the church, need an excuse to leave it. However, others will (I believe) see past the paucity of arguments and come through stronger in their faith than when they first confronted those arguments—as I did. I was firmly convinced of the truth of our 1844 teaching before I started writing *Graffiti in the Holy of Holies.* Now, having finished, I am more convinced than ever.

My hope and prayer is that those who finish *Graffiti in the Holy of Holies* will have a similar experience. If so, my efforts are more than rewarded.

1 Ellen White, *Selected Messages,* book 3, pp. 277, 278.
2 Ellen White, *Testimonies for the Church,* vol. 4, pp. 635–637.
3 For a fuller treatment of the Reform Dress issue, see Francis Nichols, *Ellen White and Her Critics* (Review and Herald; Takoma Park, Washington, DC) 1951 pp. 136–160.
4 Walter T. Rea, *The White Lie* (Turlock, Calif.: M & R Publications, 1982).
5 Ellen White, *Testimonies for the Church,* vol. 2, p. 400; *Counsels on Diet and Foods,* pp. 203, 204.
6 Ellen White, *Ministry of Healing,* p. 302; *Selected Messages,* book 3, p. 287.
7 George Knight, *Reading Ellen White* (Review and Herald; Hagerstown, MD) 1997.
8 *CDSDA,* p.106.
9 *Ibid.,* Preface [13].
10 *Ibid.,* p. 83.
11 *Ibid.,* p. 235.
12 *Ibid.,* p. 43.
13 *Ibid.,* p. 44. "It should be noted here that EGW's endorsement of Miller's conclusion came *after* 1844 when it should have been obvious that Miller was wrong."
14 *Ibid.,* p. 93, n. 18.
15 Ellen White, *Spiritual Gifts,* vol. 1, p. 128, quoted in *CDSDA,* p. 45.
16 *Ibid.,* pp. 131, 132, quoted in *CDSDA.*
17 Ellen White, *The Great Controversy,* p. 22.
18 Ellen White, *Early Writings,* p. 74, quoted in *CDSDA,* p. 84.
19 *Ibid.,* quoted in *CDSDA,* p. 234.
20 Ellen White, *A Word to the Little Flock,* 1847.
21 *CDSDA,* p. 121.
22 Ellen White, *Selected Messages,* book 1, pp. 62–65.
23 Ellen White, *Early Writings,* p. 42.
24 *Ibid.,* p. iv.
25 *CDSDA,* p. 318.
26 *Ibid.,* p. 226.
27 *Ibid.*
28 *Ibid.,* p. 321.
29 *Ibid.,* p. 337.
30 *Ibid.,* p. 321.
31 Ellen White, *Manuscript Releases,* vol. 3, pp. 420, 421 (Ms. 36, 1890).
32 Ellen White, *Faith and Works,* p. 20.
33 Ellen White, *Selected Messages* book, 1, p. 351.
34 *Ibid.,* p. 398.
35 Ellen White, *A New Life,* p. 26.
36 Ellen White, *In Heavenly Places,* p. 23.
37 Ellen White, *Testimonies for the Church,* vol. 8, p. 125.
38 Ellen White, *Faith and Works,* pp. 99, 100.
39 Ellen White, *Selected Messages,* book 1, p. 392.
40 Ellen White, *God's Amazing Grace,* p. 265.
41 Ellen White, *Selected Messages,* book 1, p. 389.
42 Ellen White, *The Desire of Ages,* p. 317.
43 *CDSDA,* p. 351.
44 *Ibid.,* Foreword [7].

# If you enjoyed this book, you'll enjoy these others by Clifford Goldstein:

### 1844 Made Simple

What significance, if any does the year 1844 and the oft attacked events surrounding it have for Christians today? From a man who came unbearably close to denying the validity of an investigative judgment and leaving the church that taught it, comes the boldest, most simple explanation and ringing endorsement of this paramount biblical teaching. Clifford Goldstein reveals the truth about 1844 and the investigative judgment in stunning clarity and unashamed passion.

0-8163-0798-9. Paperback. US$8.99, Can$13.49.

### The Great Compromise

In what many will call his most provocative and poignant work to date, Clifford Goldstein exposes what is perhaps the greatest compromise of biblical truth to take place in Christian history. With the skill of a prosecutor, Goldstein reveals:

• How evangelicals are compromising the most precious truth of justification by faith alone for political purposes.

• The documents that conservative evangelicals are using to "heal the deadly wound" with Rome.

• How the Antichrist is unmistakably revealed in *The Catechism*—and why evangelicals are ignoring it!

0-8163-1821-2. US$10.99, Can$16.49.

### Like a Fire in My Bones

*Clifford Goldstein*. The author's most important and passionate messages. The best of what he has written over the last 20 years touches on topics such as end times, religious persecution, the judgment, and more.

0-8163-1580-9. Paperback. US$6.97, Can$10.47.

Order from your ABC by calling **1-800-765-6955**, or get online and shop our virtual store at **www.AdventistBookCenter.com**.

• Read a chapter from your favorite book
• Order online
• Sign up for email notices on new products

Prices subject to change without notice.